會與

美國國國目
圖書館編
主題

陳麥麟屏・林國強 著

三民書局印行

圖書資訊學叢書

國家圖書館出版品預行編目資料

美國國會圖書館與主題編目 ／ 陳麥麟屏, 林國強
著. -- 增訂二版一刷. -- 臺北市：三民, 民90
　　面；　　公分
參考書目：面
含索引
ISBN 957-14-3336-5（平裝）

1. 標題 － 英國語言 2. 編目 － 英國語言

023.473　　　　　　　　　　　　89017974

網路書店位址　http://www.sanmin.com.tw

© 美國國會圖書館與主題編目

著作人　陳麥麟屏　林國強
發行人　劉振強
著作財　三民書局股份有限公司
產權人　臺北市復興北路三八六號
發行所　三民書局股份有限公司
　　　　地址／臺北市復興北路三八六號
　　　　電話／二五〇〇六六〇〇
　　　　郵撥／〇〇〇九九九八——五號
印刷所　三民書局股份有限公司
門市部　復北店／臺北市復興北路三八六號
　　　　重南店／臺北市重慶南路一段六十一號
初版一刷　中華民國七十八年十二月
增訂二版一刷　中華民國九十年一月
　編　號　S 02003
行政院新聞局登記證局版臺業字第〇二〇〇號

有著作權·不准侵害

ISBN　957-14-3336-5　（平裝）

編者的話

　　當我在草擬這叢書的書名時，一位在唸圖書資訊學的同學曾建議我用「圖書資訊科學」做書名，她的意思很明顯：(1)她認為「圖書資訊學」是一種「科學」；(2)用了「科學」兩個字，便可以在一般社會人士心目中提高這門學問的身價，因而便可使更多人願意學習這門學問，而獻身圖書資訊事業。這位同學的看法，不但反映了一般社會人士對「圖書資訊學」的看法，也多多少少說出了她自己和很多圖書資訊從業人員的心態。這個普及的心態來源有自，背景很是複雜。簡單的說，一方面是因為近百年來自然科學在社會進化過程中的衝擊性；另一方面，是因為從事圖書資訊事業的人們對這門學問的認識有偏差，我很能瞭解並同情這個建議。考慮再三，我仍然用「圖書資訊學」做書名，我覺得，「學」字本身便已經有了「系統化研求」的涵義，而且在一般社會人士的心目中，既然已將「科學」二字當作「自然科學」的專用詞，又何必在已經複雜已極的現代名詞中，為大家更增添不必要的混淆？巴特勒(Pierce Butler)先生說得好：「不管如何，一個詞的意義決定在社會的採納與否，而不在邏輯性地下定義。」❶再說回頭，要改變一般社會人士對這門學問的看法，不是硬用「科學」一詞便可以達到的，一切還得看這門學問是不是值得人們冠以「科學」這個詞，還得看我

---

❶ Butler, Pierce, *An Introduction to Library Science* ,Chicago: University of Chicago Press, 1933, p. 2.

們從事這項事業的人是否值得人們重視。我感謝這位同學的建議，但也不想為不採納這個建議而致歉。

知識的成長是社會進步的原動力，而圖書資訊卻是知識成長必備的要素。知識是人們日積月累的經驗和研究的成果，這些知識的結晶便儲藏在圖書資訊中。圖書資訊學是研究：

①、目前及以往圖書資訊的型態；

②、蒐集它們的方法；

③、整理它們的過程和方法；以及

④、傳播它們到需求者的方式、過程和途徑。

根據上述四項研究成果來改進一切圖書資訊的作業程序，並推測、試擬未來圖書資訊作業的方向與方法，所以，我們也可以說圖書資訊學是社會進步、文化發揚的基石。

參照國內需求，這套叢書先出十二本作第一輯：

①、《圖書資訊學導論》　　　　　　周寧森著

②、《資訊政策》　　　　　　　　　張鼎鍾著

③、《圖書資訊之組織與原理》　　　何光國著

④、《圖書資訊之儲存及檢索》　　　張庭國著

⑤、《圖書館之管理及組織》　　　　李華偉著

⑥、《圖書館際合作與資訊網之建設》林孟真著

⑦、《美國國會圖書館主題編目》　　陳麥麟屏、林國強合著

⑧、《圖書館與當代資訊科技》　　　景懿頻著

⑨、《圖書資訊學專業教育》　　　　沈寶環著

⑩、《法律圖書館》　　　　　　　　夏道泰著

⑪、《文獻計量學導論》　　　　　　何光國著

⑫、《圖書館學理論基礎》　　　　　何光國著

　　本叢書的作者都是當代圖書資訊學的精英，內容均能推陳出新，深入淺出，特地在此向他們致最高的敬意和最深的謝意，若有疏漏之處，都是編者一人的責任。

　　最後，我要向三民書局劉振強先生致敬，像這樣專業性的學術叢書是注定了要蝕本的，劉先生為了國家民族的遠景，毅然斥資去做這項明知無利可圖但影響深遠的事，實在不由人不佩服。

周寧森

於新澤西州

周　序

　　我認識麥麟屏(Lois Mai Chan)教授已經四十餘年，但在臺大讀書時，她是高我一年的學姐，平日不苟言笑，我們並不熟悉，只知道她是外文系的高材生，因為「書卷」榜上有名。

　　後在紐約（大約是1958年），麟屏與內子彭小玉曾共度一段「流美」的艱苦日子。1963年，我們在芝加哥結婚，她不遠千里趕來，擔當伴娘，算來也是36年前的事了。之後，她在佛州州立大學攻得文學及圖書館學碩士，在肯塔基大學獲得比較文學博士，並在肯大圖書資訊學院教學至今，已是美國圖書館學界主題標目學的權威了。

　　林國強(James K. Lin)博士曾任職於美國國會圖書館近20年，是國會圖書館的主題編目專家，對主題編目之實際作業極為嫻熟，對館內組織之嬗遞演變亦知之甚詳。林君目前任職哈佛大學哈佛—燕京圖書館。此書匯集二位豐富的專業知識並由林君執筆，實為《圖書資訊學叢書》增色不少。

　　此書前三章簡介美國國會圖書館及其業務，四至八章介紹主題編目之理論與實際作業，第九章描述美國國會圖書館內之各種自動化系統以及它們的範圍，兼及美國研究圖書館組織(RLG)和(OCLC)的中、日、韓文(CJK)資料自動化處理系統，第十章更列舉主題編目作業中各種工具書。

　　本書經著者增刪之後，較原版更為完善，不但為一般讀者清晰地

勾畫出美國國會圖書館的型態及其各種作業，並能為圖書館業者深入淺出、婉轉地道出主題編目的立論根據，行文更是流暢、簡約，是一本極好的參考讀物。

周寧森

1999於新澤西州

增訂二版序言

美國國會圖書館的圖書分類法和主題編目制度，已有百年左右的歷史淵源。它們廣泛地為美國國內以及世界各地大型圖書館所採用，是圖書資訊學從業者以及學生不可不熟悉的制度。

遺憾的是過去並沒有一部以中文撰述美國國會圖書館主題編目制度的專著，1989年出版的《美國國會圖書館主題編目》一書適足以彌補這項缺失。

該書出版以來，承臺灣各圖書館系所採用為教科書。作者訪問香港，北京，以及美國圖書館時，也常邂逅閱讀本書的編目工作人員。彼此交換意見，相得益彰。

作者在1999年依據1989年版做大幅度的增訂。其中增加介紹國會圖書館改組後的新面貌，及其現階段的任務，與原書的主要議題：主題編目，構成新書的兩大議題。有鑑於此，本書書名也因而改為《美國國會圖書館與主題編目》。

本書的主旨有二。它一方面介紹世界第一大圖書館——美國國會圖書館，它的歷史淵源、組織、功能，以及其現階段任務。另一方面闡述美國國會圖書館主題編目制度的理論，以及實際業務的執行。作者無意在此臧否美國國會圖書館的主題編目制度，亦不擬比較它和其他主題編目制度的優劣。書中列舉的編目例子，都是美國國會圖書館實際編目的成例。所引用的標題也完全採擷於現行的《美國國會圖書

館主題標目表》(*Library of Congress Subject Headings*)。為了行文方便，不再個別註明出處。

　　從1989年的《美國國會圖書館主題編目》一書的出版到1999年增訂的《美國國會圖書館與主題編目》，足足有10年之久。這10年間，國會圖書館經歷大幅度的改組。本書反映它改組後的新面目。主題編目的細節變化甚多。要而言之，是逐漸地走向規章簡單化，條目統一化的目標，以便利編目與檢索。

　　本書失誤疏漏之處，請來函指正，以便於新版時修訂。

林國強　陳麥麟屏

1999年6月於美國，劍橋，哈佛大學

目　次

第一章　美國國會圖書館的昨日與今日

一、草創之過程

美國國會圖書館(Library of Congress)創立於1800年4月24日。其目的是在新建立的國會山莊裡提供一個特別為國會議員們服務的圖書館[1]。

第一批經由美國第六任總統 John Adams 簽署撥款的經費是：$5,000元。一部分作為在國會大廈內裝設圖書室的費用，另一部分用來購置圖書。初期的圖書完全選購自英國[2]。從1800年到1812年的12年期間，國會圖書館的圖書庋藏總數僅得3,000冊左右[3]。也就是說，美國國會圖書館草創之初，侷促在國會大廈的一隅，談不上任何規模建制，藏書也貧乏得可憐。

這種篳路藍縷、慘澹經營的局面，僅維持了14年。1814年8月英軍進兵華府(Washington, D.C.)，把國會大廈付之一炬。其中的圖書館

---

[1] Library of Congress,*Guide to the Library of Congress* (Washington, D. C.: Library of Congress, 1985), p. 3.

[2] Gail Sakurai, *Cornerstones of Freedom: The Library of Congress* (New York: Grolier Publishing, 1998), p. 3.

[3] 同[1], p. 4。

藏書也成灰燼。

　　業已退休的美國第三任總統湯瑪斯・傑佛遜 (Thomas Jefferson) 聞悉圖書慘遭兵燹，主動建議把他50年苦心經營的6,487部圖書轉讓給國會。這些庋藏，是當時新大陸最豐盛的藏書，內容包羅萬象。他認為：「國會圖書館的圖書，必需網羅齊全，囊括所有的知識。因為國會議員們將來需要研究參考的議題，是無法事先設限的。」 ❹ 國會乃於1815年1月以$23,950元購買了 Jefferson 的書籍，作為重建國會圖書館藏書的基礎 ❺。誰能預料到竟從此發展成為世界上最宏偉的圖書館呢？而 Jefferson 「廣博精深」的建議，乃成為日後國會圖書館奉行的圭臬。論者推崇 Jefferson 為美國圖書館界之父，可謂實至名歸。

二、今日的美國國會圖書館

　　無論從庋藏數目論，或從圖書館的建築規模而論，今天的美國國會圖書館均不愧是世界首屈一指的圖書館。它在國會山莊的主要建築有三，最古老的一幢，Thomas Jefferson Building，是為紀念 Jefferson 總統對國會圖書館的貢獻而命名的。它是一幢義大利文藝復興時代式樣的建築，完成於1897年。外觀莊嚴恢宏，氣勢磅礴，內部則雕樑畫棟，雍容華貴，是匯集50位當代名匠經年累月的心血結晶。然而經過近百年的歲月推移，建築內部日漸浸損，設備也不敷使用，直到1980年最新的一幢建築 James Madison Memorial Building 竣工啟用，才將這幢元老建築的大部分功能取而代之。1986年 Jefferson Building 進行

---

❹　同❷, p. 2。

❺　同❷, p. 5。

大規模的整修工作。歷經11年,於1997年5月1日竣工,重新開放使用 ❻。亞洲研究部也自此從 John Adams Building 遷入該館。這是美國最具有歷史性的建築物之一,也是華府最吸引遊客的地方。美國歷史雖僅短短兩百餘年,而其勠力保存和維護文化資產的決心是值得推崇的。

第二幢建築,John Adams Building,落成於1939年。這一幢大理石建築,可以「樸實」兩字形容它。對使用中文圖書者而言,它是中文藏書的所在,也是世界上除了中國本土之外最大的中文收藏所。其中又以中國地方誌、叢書和族譜的收集彌足珍貴。

James Madison Memorial Building,這幢最新的建築落成於1980年,其面積超過前面兩幢建築的總合,是華府數一數二的巨無霸。它的到來,使日漸擁擠不堪的國會圖書館,暫時得到了舒緩。這三幢建築的地板(floor space)總面積有71英畝。

此外,國會圖書館還有座落在國內外的其他分支單位。目前在國外的單位有6個,它們分別座落於:開羅(Cairo)、雅加達(Jakarta)、喀拉蚩(Karachi)、奈洛比(Nairobi)、新德里(New Delhi)、里約熱內盧(Rio de Janeiro) ❼。

整個國會圖書館的收藏超過1億個項目。如果把書架以直線排列,可以綿延532英里。而它正以每天增加7,000個項目的驚人速度不斷的擴展。它擁有2,900萬本書,5,300萬冊手稿(manuscript),400萬冊地圖集(atlas),600萬冊樂譜及音樂家的手稿,1,500萬冊的圖片,

---

❻ Library of Congress: ***Thomas Jefferson Building*** (Washington, D.C.: Library of Congress, 1997), p. 24.

❼ Library of Congress, Processing Services, ***Statistical Highlights*** (Washington, D.C.: Library of Congress, 1988), p. 1.

Thomas Jefferson Building

John Adams Building

James Madison Memorial Building

Thomas Jefferson　大樓前廊（Michael Dersin攝製）

Thomas Jefferson　大樓的閱覽室一角（Jim Higgins攝製）

Thomas Jefferson　大樓閱覽室的雕樑畫壁（Bela L. Pratt攝製）

以上圖片資料，承蒙美國國會圖書館公共事務 Helen Dalrymple 小姐的鼎力協助，獲得原圖片製作者同意轉載。謹此致謝。

350萬張唱片和錄音資料(sound recording)，25萬卷影片(motion picture)，600萬份以上的縮形膠卷(microform)。每年還有75,000種定期刊物，一千二百多份報紙如潮水般的湧進 ❽ 。

國會圖書館早年的收藏以美國文明為重心，歐洲文明也佔重要地位，亞非收藏並不受重視。這種重美歐，輕亞非的觀點，到了第二次世界大戰以後才有顯著的轉變。以中文收藏為例，從1869年與滿清政府交換933冊中文圖書開始，中文圖書收藏的進度頗為遲滯，並且沒有適當的編目。直到60年代以後中文圖書收藏才開始有顯著的增加，而編目工作也逐漸系統化。1986和1987兩年間國會圖書館從中國大陸、香港、臺灣三個地區，以購買、交換及贈送方式得到的中文書籍有53,596冊，其增加數量僅次於英文書籍 ❾ 。它已儼然成為中國地區以外的中文庋藏重鎮。

國會圖書館在1981年開始採用電腦機讀式目錄，取代了卡片式的目錄。

目前館內的書籍(book)約有四分之一是英語，其他的書籍包括世界上470種語言。其收藏方向，與美國國家的世界觀亦步亦趨。

國會圖書館館長(Librarian)需由總統提名，國會同意而任命。從1800年成立以來，共經歷13位館長。第一任館長是由 Jefferson 總統提名而於1802年就任的 James Beckly。現任館長 James H. Billington，是由雷根總統提名，於1987年9月14日就任迄今。

國會圖書館現有員工四千餘人。目前的主要任務依其優先秩序是 ❿：

---

❽ 同❷，p. 3。

❾ Library of Congress, *Library of Congress Information Bulletin* (Washington, D.C.: Library of Congress , February 8, 1988), pp. 57–58.

第一：對美國國會提供最新和最可靠的分析資料。

第二：有系統地收藏，保存、整理有關美國歷史以及世界其他地方的知識文件。

第三：通過「國家圖書數據計劃」(National Digital Library Program)把智庫傳播，提供給國會、政府機構，以及廣大群眾。

第四：有效地利用收藏品做為教育性，啟發性的媒介物。

美國國會圖書館在短短200年的時間，從僅有六千餘冊藏書的小型圖書館發展到美國國家性的圖書館，再一躍而成為睨視寰宇的世界性圖書館。它服務的對象，從少年到老年，從盲人到坐輪椅者。服務的地區亦無遠弗屆，每年從全世界各地來訪的人數多達250萬人。它的最高宗旨是：「匯集全球知識於一室，俾使其成為解決任何問題的鎖鑰。」⓫

⓾　Library of Congress, *25 Questions most Frequently Asked by Visitor* (Washington D.C.: Library of Congress, 1997), p. 3.

⓫　同⓾，p. 1。

第二章　美國國會圖書館的組織

美國國會圖書館的最高負責人是館長。館長是終身職，由總統提名，經國會同意後任命。美國國會圖書館直接由國會議員組成的特別委員會負責監督其業務。

館長之下有6個主要的部門，見表2-1

一、行政機構(Enabling Infrastructure)

這是管理整個圖書館的行政業務單位。下轄財務、人事、資訊技術、整合支援、計劃考核、安全等單位。

二、國會研究部(Congressional Research Service)

它保存了國會圖書館創立的初衷，即對國會議員提供直接的服務。議員們可以把議事工作有關的事項，譬如準備聽證背景資料，彙編辯論意見，分析立法提案，研究政策議題，評估司法裁決等交由這個單位負責研究，並限期擬定回覆。簡單的問題可能僅需短短幾行或幾頁的回覆，可以在幾小時或一兩天之內完成任務。複雜的問題則需要長時間的研究，而其回覆可能長達幾百頁，譬如裁軍問題、預算問

表2-1　美國國會圖書館組織

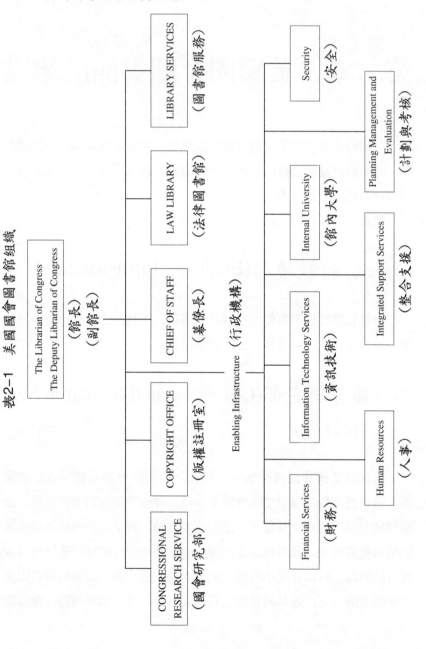

題及環境衛生問題等。這個單位不受黨派或行政當局左右，它對問題的立場力求客觀，它不對問題直接提出解決方案，而是從各種角度做深入的探索，把所有可能的解決辦法一一提交給議員，讓他們自行從中取捨。這部門的專家分屬以下9個單位：

1. 美國法律處(American Law Division)
2. 國會查詢處(Congressional Reference Division)
3. 經濟處(Economics Division)
4. 教育及公共福利處(Education and Public Welfare Division)
5. 環境及自然資源政策處(Environment and Natural Resources Policy Division)
6. 外交與國家資源政策(Foreign Affairs and National Resources Policy)
7. 政府(Government)
8. 圖書館服務(Library Services)
9. 科技與醫藥(Science, Technology and Medicine)

三、法律圖書館(Law Library)

這個單位擁有美國最完善的歐美法律藏書。除了歐美法律部(Western Law Division)，它還設有東方法律部(Eastern Law Division)。一般民眾可以到此借用書刊，但只限館內使用。個人不得借出書刊。

四、版權註冊室(Copyright Office)

它處理美國版權註冊。版權不限於書刊，舉凡音樂、劇本、舞臺設計、雕刻、電影、圖片、繪畫、錄音資料、電腦程式、地圖、建築設計藍圖等屬於智慧產品都是版權註冊的範疇。

五、圖書館服務(Library Services)

它有以下的單位:

1. 保存(Preservation)。　它的業務包括研究保存圖書的技術。修護、複印、裝訂圖書等事項。

2. 地區研究收藏(Area Studies Collections)。　它的地區研究包括:

(1)非洲與中東處(African and Middle Eastern Division)

(2)亞洲處(Asian Division)

(3)歐洲處(European Division)

(4)聯邦研究處(Federal Research Division)

(5)西班牙語系處(Hispanic Division)

(6)學術研究計劃室(Office of Scholarly Programs)

3. 採購及供應服務(Acquisition and Support Services)。　它包括以下的單位:

(1)非洲／亞洲採購及海外作業處(African/Asian Acquisitions and Overseas Operation Division)

(2)英美採購處(Anglo-American Acquisitions Division)

(3)歐洲／拉丁美洲採購處(European/Latin American Acquisitions Division)

(4)採購財務處(Acquisitions Fiscal Office)

(5)網路發展及機讀式目錄標準室(Network Development and MARC Standards Office)

(6)期刊處(Serial Record Division)

(7)作業技術及自動化教導室(Technical Processing and Automation Iustruction Office)

4.全國性的服務(National Services)。 它包括:

(1)目錄發售服務(Cataloging Distribution Services)

(2)圖書服務中心(Center for the Book)

(3)聯邦圖書館和資訊中心委員會(Federal Library and Information Center Committee)

(4)國家數據圖書館(National Digital Library)

(5)全國盲人及身體殘障者圖書服務中心(National Library Services for the Blind and Physically Handicapped)

(6)出版室(Publishing Office)

5.公共服務收藏(Public Service Collections) 它包括以下數種服務單位:

(1)美國民俗中心(American Folklore Center)

(2)兒童文學中心(Children's Literature Center)

(3)地理及地圖處(Geography and Map Division)

(4)人文及社會科學處(Humanities and Social Sciences Division)

(5)借書處(Loan Division)

(6)手稿處(Manuscript Division)

(7)影片、廣播及錄音資料處(Motion Picture, Broadcasting and Recorded Sound Division)

(8)音樂處(Music Division)

(9)全國查詢服務(National Reference Service)

(10)圖片及影像處(Prints and Photograph Division)

(11)珍本書籍及特別收藏處(Rare Book and Special Collections Division)

(12)期刊及政府出版品處(Serial and Government Publications Division)

(13)藏書管理處(Collections Management Division)

六、編目部(Cataloging Directorate)

這個部門與本書的內容最為相關。主題編目就是編目部門的一項重要作業。它的單位有:

1.編目策劃及技援室(Cataloging Policy and Support Office)。這是負責訂定編目規範及解釋編目條文的單位,也是編目部的靈魂中心。它定期出版以下重要的編目工具書,以供應世界各地使用國會圖書館編目制度者。

(1)國會圖書館主題標目表(*Library of Congress Subject Headings*)

(2)標題標準檔(*Subject Authority File*)

(3)著錄標準檔(*Descriptive Authority File*)

(4)國會圖書館規章詮釋(*Library of Congress Rule Interpretations*)

(5)編目服務公報(*Cataloging Service Bulletin*)

(6)主題編目手冊(*Subject Cataloging Manuals*)。手冊包括主題標

目 (Subject Headings)、 分 類 (Classification) 以 及 排 架 目 錄 (Shelflisting)三種。

(7)國會圖書館分類表(*Library of Congress Classification Schedules*)

2.**待出版書編目處(Cataloging in Publication Division)。** 所有將在美國出版的書籍，在出版之前將稿件寄送到國會圖書館版權處申請版權。在這同時，編目部也依據稿本進行編目工作。是以書籍印製出版後其目錄也出現在書名頁之後。這些書內現成的目錄（包括分類號）就是這個單位的成品。目前許多書商利用電腦將整個稿件輸送到國會圖書館。而國會圖書館也利用電腦將版權資料、目錄輸回給書商。比以前郵件寄送稿件快捷方便甚多。

3.**十進位分類處(Decimal Classification Division)。** 目前還有許多圖書館採用杜威(Dewey)創製的十進位分類法。為了方便這些圖書館，此單位在國會目錄上除了提供國會圖書館分類法之外，也同時提供十進位分類法。

4.**藝術及科學編目處(Arts and Sciences Cataloging Division)。** 它細分為以下各組：

(1)美術、建築及藝術表演組(Art, Architecture, and Performing Arts Team)

(2)生物及農業科學組(Biological and Agricultural Sciences Team)

(3)醫學及生物工學組(Medical Sciences and Biotechnology Team)

(4)物理科學組(Physical Sciences Team)

(5)應用科學組(Technology Team)

5.**歷史及文學編目處(History and Literature Cataloging Division)**

(1)英美組(Anglo-American Team)

⑵兒童文學組(Children's Literature Team)

⑶一般歷史及文學組(General History and Literature Team)

⑷德語系歷史及文學組(Germanic History and Literature Team)

⑸西班牙語系歷史及文學組(Hispanic History and Literature Team)

⑹羅馬語系歷史及文學組(Romance History and Literature Team)

⑺斯拉夫語系歷史及文學組(Slavic History and Literature Team)

6.社會科學編目處(Social Sciences Cataloging Division)

⑴商業及經濟組(Business and Economics Team)

⑵中歐東歐語文組(Central and Eastern European Languages Team)

⑶教育、體育及娛樂組(Education, Sports, and Recreation Team)

⑷德語系及斯勘地那維亞語系組(Germanic and Scandinavian Languages Team)

⑸法律組(Law Team)

⑹政治學、社會學及人類學組(Political Science, Sociology, and Anthropology Team)

⑺宗教、哲學及心理學組(Religion, Philosophy, and Psychology Team)

⑻羅馬語系組(Romance Languages Team)

7.特殊資料編目處(Special Materials Cataloging Division)

⑴電腦文件、微形膠卷組(Computer Files/Microforms Team)

⑵音樂及錄音資料組(Music and Sound Recordings Team)

⑶珍本書組(Rare Book Team)

8.區域及合作編目處(Regional and Cooperative Cataloging Division)。 區域編目負責亞洲和北非區域的編目。前面所提幾個編目處是以「主題」為依據,再以語文細分為組。特殊資料編目處是以

「資料」為分組之對象，而這裡是以「區域」為編目劃分的依據。中、日、韓等語文的書籍，不論其主題，全部均屬這個部門編目。它有以下幾個亞非語文組：

　1. 中文組(Chinese Team)

　2. 韓文組(Korean Team)。它目前也負責一部份中文編目。

　3. 日文組(Japanese Team)

　4. 希伯來語組(Hebraica Team)

　5. 中東／北非組(Middle East/North Africa Team)

　6. 南亞組(South Asia Team)

　7. 東南亞組(Southeast Asia Team)。它目前也負責一部分南亞書籍的編目。

　　除此之外，這個編目處還有一項非常特殊的任務，這就是所謂「合作編目」(Cooperative Cataloging)。它是由合作編目組(Cooperative Cataloging Team)來負責。

　　合作編目是目前美國圖書館館際一項最重要的編目作業，研讀美國圖書館作業者不可不知，我們因此特別在下一章專門介紹合作編目的由來和其結構。

第三章　美國館際合作編目計劃

一、合作編目的由來

　　1995年成立的「合作編目計劃」(Program for Cooperative Cataloging，簡稱 PCC) 是國會圖書館從事館際合作業務25年來經驗的累積。國會圖書館最早的一項館際合作業務是1973年創立的「連線期刊合作計劃」(Cooperative Online Serials Program，簡稱CONSER)。1977年「名稱標準檔合作計劃」(Name Authority Cooperative Program，簡稱 NACO) 接著開始運作。它的任務是館際聯合發展「國家名稱標準檔」(包括叢書名稱)。其後，國會圖書館又展開「全國協調合作計劃」(National Coordinated Cooperative Program，簡稱 NCCP)。它的任務是聯合其他12個圖書館依據編目規範，分別製作完整書目(tull-level record)，輸入共同的資料庫。使參與的圖書館能分享更多的書目資源，並且避免編目的重複。

　　「合作編目計劃」顧名思義，是一個合作協調的機構。大部分的會員有投票權。行政委員會的成員包括國會圖書館、英國圖書館、加拿大國家圖書館、美國國家醫藥圖書館、圖書館收藏及技術服務協會(美國圖書館協會的分支)。國會圖書館同時也是該計劃的祕書處，負責日常業務。行政委員會督導該計劃的策略，建立標準，促進圖書館之間的聯絡，以及籌募基金。

行政委員會在會員中任命兩位編目作執行顧問。這兩位有經驗的編目員負責對行政委員會提供編目趨勢，以及新技術的發展。

此外，還有三個小組：行政委員會、執行顧問、常設小組，提供基本的政策，規劃與執行業務。國會圖書館擔起祕書處的責任。它是合作編目計劃不可缺少的棟樑。有了它，整個計劃才能活絡地執行它的既定目標。祕書處提供行政委員會活動場所，延攬新會員，負責培訓工作，擬訂文件，聯絡參與圖書館，收集和研判資料。總而言之，它負責推行合作編目計劃的使命與目標。國會圖書館的編目總監同時也是行政委員會的永久會員。自創始迄今編目總監一直被會員推選為該會的主席。國會圖書館的「區域和合作編目處」(RCCD)主任充當主席顧問，也是祕書處日常業務的實際執行人。此外國會圖書館的幾位編目員和技術員經常輔助祕書處業務，和參與人事交流，推廣宣傳業務。

二、合作編目的目標

合作編目計劃是為了實現「多」、「快」、「好」、「省」的四項目標。

先從「多」上來講，要增加書目的數量。1995年國會圖書館製作235,000件完整書目(full-level record)；43,000件最簡略書目(minimal-level record)；114,000件標準名稱和標準叢書檔；8,902件標準主題目錄檔。以上的產量比5年前增加15％，而工作人員卻相對的減少大約20％。這種業績誠難能可貴。

此外，我們還必需提到參與會員的貢獻。該計劃最主要任務之一是擴充會員。因為參與者眾，生產的數量自然提高。該計劃希望會員

分擔編目工作，根據本身能力，擬定每年生產數量，如此就不至於使
少數會員分攤過多責任。該計劃擬訂在公元2000年前每年增產80,000
件書目，以及150,000件標準目錄檔。

該計劃成立迄今一直不斷的在成長中：從1992年到1997年，
NACO從66,000件增加到92,000件。其中叢書和主題標準名稱檔，被
認為是最難製作的一部分，在這其間，增加300％。

一項新的計劃，合作從事一般編目輸入工作，簡稱為 BIBCO，
剛開始進行不久。這項計劃預計每年能夠生產15,000件一般書目。幾
所規模大的圖書館正全力投入這項計劃 ❶。

編目員和使用者一致認為在求多的過程中，絕對不能忽視品質的
重要性。

為了降低成本，美國許多圖書館複製其他圖書館現成的目錄。這
種風氣已流傳許久，但自1990年代以來，複製更為普及。就以國會圖
書館為例，1992年國會圖書館只複製1,800件別人的書目，到了1997
年它的複製書目增加到54,000件。有了 BIBCO 計劃，複製就更簡便
了。

複製品一定要符合編目規範，才能採用，否則徒增麻煩。有鑑於
此，PCC 訂定規範，要求會員遵守，以免劣品質的製品流入資料
庫。

為了維持一定的標準，美國圖書館界近來議定了一項稱為「基礎
書目」(core-level record)的編目規範。什麼是基礎書目呢？它的款目
比最簡略書目的內容充實，但不及完整書目來得詳細。

「基礎書目」具有完備的書目說明，具有電腦的固定字段符號，

---

❶ *Program for Cooperative Cataloging* (Washington D.C.: Library of
Congress, Program for Cooperative Cataloging Home Page, 1998), pp. 2–7.

包括一到二項主題標目，以便檢索並提供標準分類號碼。然而它可以不加註解，也可以不加次要的款目。 PCC的會員准許以基礎書目方法來編目，也可以完整書目方法來編目，由會員自己做選擇。

「基礎書目」的規範目前已經訂定完成，可以用來做下列各種資料的編目：書籍、期刊、樂譜、錄音資料、視聽資料，和非羅馬字的出版品。

PCC 接受基礎編目法。其他圖書館可視需要而加添款目。

在當今電子化的時代，書籍的出版大量增加。編目工作，除了講求「更多」和「更好」之外，另一項需要考慮的課題是經濟的負擔。國會圖書館編目部門除了要應付每天新進的書刊，還得應付庫存裡尚待編目的書籍。PCC 一再強調低成本，高效率方法的重要性。

為了講求多與好，又要做到快與省的目標，可行的方法是積極培訓編目員，以期編目員能夠儘快達到獨立自主，不怕嘗試，而具有判斷力的境界。PCC 在培訓編目員時，特別強調要在多好與快省之間做平衡的估量。稱得上好品質的編目，也必須是講究時效的。過去至少有20位編目員在 PCC 培訓時，被灌輸了這些觀念。希望他們把所學帶回到他們工作機構去影響其他的編目人員。

在規範上簡化，也對求快與省有直接的助益。

PCC 的行政委員會認為編目規範必需朝簡化的方向走。國會圖書館秉承此意，已經簡化30條規範說明，並完全取消4條。國會圖書館的主標題目也朝簡化方向走，將來的編目工作會容易些。

三、合作編目的效益

參與「合作編目計劃」(PCC)、「連線期刊合作計劃」(CONSER)

以及其他的合作項目，有許多好處：

1.可以在電腦資料庫中接觸更多的國內外書目及標準目錄檔。資料庫愈豐富，編目愈容易。

2.更可靠的編目：規範的訂定提高了書目的品質。

3.更有效的編目：圖書館可以擬定新的工作流程，以便利複印其他圖書館的書目。這些工作可以交給技術員去做。

4.更節省時間的編目：複印現成的書目比自己做要快得多。

5.低成本高效率的編目：大家合作編目，一定比獨立編目要省事、省錢。

6.通過連機網路更容易解決編目問題。

7.能夠得到專家的培訓：國會圖書館和其他機構可以提供培訓編目員。這些受過訓的人員本身又可成為訓練人。

8.對國內外的編目政策產生影響力：參加 PCC 和 CONSER 的會員有權參與擬定，修改規範。而這些規範對英美編目規則以及國會圖書館的規範解釋有直接影響力。

9.編目人員省下的時間可以用在其他活動上：目前電腦資訊日益重要，圖書館職員在傳統書刊編目中節省下來的時間、金錢，可以轉用在新興的電腦資訊傳達上。

四、國會圖書館與國際合作編目

在國際合作編目的領域中，國會圖書館的領導地位是顯而易見的。它擁有世界最大的書目資料庫，它以 PCC 與 CONSER 為據點，戮力推行國際合作計劃。在1990年代新技術和國際間編目規範漸趨一

致之際，國會圖書館正努力嘗試聯繫更多的外語資料庫和標準檔，以便利使用。

PCC 邀請英國圖書館、加拿大圖書館加入 PCC 並成為執行委員會的永久會員，是一項國際合作計劃成功的明證。國會圖書館和加拿大圖書館目前已把這兩個國家的機讀式目錄規範統一，合併成為一個國際機讀式目錄(MARC 21)。德國圖書館對這項計劃也深感興趣。

英國圖書館已經成功的把它們的標準名稱檔輸入 NACO。從1997年年初到目前曾輸入了3,000件以上的標準名稱檔。它預計到2000年時這項數字將會加倍。它從1993年重新使用國會圖書館主題標目表(LCSH)以來，也陸續地輸入了不少的主題標目。英國地區還有其他5、6所圖書館也是 LCSH 的提供單位。其他的參與圖書館來自蘇格蘭、威爾斯、義大利、瑞典、紐西蘭、立陶宛等國。另外南非、以色列等地區的圖書館也有意加入行列。

國會圖書館長期以來在編目上居領導地位。早年它設計的電腦機讀式目錄，一直沿用迄今。它們負責發展和維持的兩種圖書分類制度：國會圖書館分類制(L.C. Classification)，和杜威分類制(Dewey Classification)，紛紛為許多圖書館採用。許多國家也採用國會圖書館的主題標目表(LCSH)。在今天的國際領域中，國會圖書館所扮演的角色是自國際合作中找尋共同點，以解決編目存在的問題，從而商擬共同的目標和規範。國會圖書館在 PCC 和 CONSER 兩項國際合作計劃中和其他參與會員分享成功的果實。會員們定期聚會商討策略，計劃目標，擬定規範。美國國會最近重申國會圖書館是美國國家圖書館的地位，並具有負責收藏和編目的領導責任。國會圖書館也深切期待以合作編目的方法來降低成本，提高生產率。

有關新近美國館際合作的訊息都可以在稱為國會電腦網站

(Congress Web Site)上面找到(http://www.loc.gov)。其中可以直接查看到 PCC 和 CONSER 以及 NSDP 等電腦網訊息。

第四章　主題編目的理論

主題編目的理論依據，一般公認是肇基於兩本著作：

1. Cutter, Charles A., ***Rules for a Dictionary Catalog*** ❶.
2. Haykin, David Judson, ***Subject Headings: A Practical Guide***.

Cutter 的著作乃主題編目理論之發軔，而 Haykin 承其餘緒而發揚之。Haykin 在其主管任內，竭力把理論在作業上付諸實現。遺憾的是，多年來主題編目單位並沒有把作業規章整理成書，公諸於世，外界無法做有系統的了解。直到1978年 Lois Mai Chan 的《國會圖書館主題標目：原理及應用》(***Library of Congress Subject Headings: Principles and Application***)一書問世 ❷，才彌補了這個缺陷。Chan 將 Cutter, Haykin 和其他學者的理論，作條理的闡述，並將歷年來主題編目處內零星散亂的規章，擇其要者作詳細的陳述。

1984年，主題編目處(Subject Cataloging Division)出版了《主題編目手冊：主題標》(***Subject Cataloging Manual: Subject Headings***) ❸，可以視為一部官方的主題編目規章。目前主題編目規章分5大冊。這5大冊的綱目，請見附錄九，我們將在以後的篇章討論它。

---

❶ Charles A. Cutter, ***Rules for a Dictionary Catalog***, 4th. ed. (Washington, D.C.: Government Printing Office, 1904).

❷ Lois Mai Chan, ***Library of Congress Subject Headings: Principles and Application*** (Littleton, Colorado: Libraries Unlimited, 3rd. ed., 1995).

❸ Library of Congress, ***Subject Cataloging Manual: Subject Headings***, (Washington, D.C.: Library of Congress, 1984, 5th. ed., 1998).

在這一章我們將 Cutter, Haykin 和其他學者對主題編目的理論綜合簡
介於下。

一、以讀者為考慮重點(the reader as a focus) 的原則

　　Cutter 認為編目應以方便讀者為基本宗旨，雖然對編目者而言完
全硬性依照體例編目是比較簡便的辦法，但有時為了遷就讀者的習
慣，編目者必須犧牲編目的條例和邏輯❹。Haykin 把上述原則視為
「以讀者為考慮重點」的編目原則。無論是規章的運用，款目(entry)
的安排，詞句的選擇，都應從讀者的觀點出發。至於邏輯、條理、體
例等原則倒是次要 ❺。

　　Cutter 與 Haykin 的原則是顯而易解的。但是實行起來卻是困難
重重。圖書館學專家們對此議論紛紛，歸納起來，有以下數點：

　　1.讀者隨圖書館的性質和地域而有所不同。兒童圖書館的讀者是
兒童，大學圖書館的讀者是大學生、教授與研究人員，醫學圖書館的
讀者是醫學從業員，這些特殊圖書館的使用對象很容易確定，但是一
般性的圖書館，如公眾圖書館，它們的使用對象是廣大的群眾，知識
水準的差距很大，背景、職業也紛紜不一。在這種情況下如何能夠顧
慮到所有讀者的習性呢？或者說要以那一類讀者的習性為依據呢？

　　2.歷年來很多學者和圖書館做了不少研究，希望找到所謂圖書館
使用者的「共同性向」。遺憾的是迄今尚未有為大家所接受的具體成

---

❹　同❶，p. 6。

❺　David Judson Haykin, *Subject Headings: A Practical Guide* (Washing-
　　ton, D.C.: Government Printing Office, 1951), p. 7.

果。也就是說以讀者為考慮重點的編目原則，並沒有提供編目者可援以為據的科學指導原則。編目者遂往往恣意推測，造成嚴重的混淆。

3.一個適宜於某一圖書館的編目原則，有時並不適宜於其他圖書館。以美國國會圖書館為例，它是美國政府的圖書館，自然以美國為主要對象。它的主題標目和分類表(classification schedule)的發展，完全以本身的庋藏為依據。其他圖書館，尤其是外國圖書館如果依樣採用，必定有水土不服之弊，或有削足適履之憾。

4.在以電腦為主，合作編目(shared cataloging)盛行的時代，完全依據條例的編目原則，對所有參與的圖書館，都是經濟而較可行的辦法。讀者假以時日也可以逐漸習慣和接受這些編目條例。據此，Cutter 和 Haykin 兩人的觀點似有不合時宜之嫌。何況在圖書資訊急速膨脹的時代，今天的圖書館，需要處理的圖書數量，何止千百倍於 Cutter 或 Haykin 的時代。過分拘泥於每一個主題標目的適應性，就難免緩不濟急。

二、主題標目的統一原則(the principle of unity)

相同的意義或觀念，必須使用同一形式的主題標目（以後在行文中簡稱標題）來表示。一個意念往往可以用多種同義語(synonymous term)，或者不同的形式(form)來表達。甚至相同的意念，因地域、風俗習慣之差別，而有不同的稱謂。主題編目者在這些情況下，必須選擇一個代表性的詞語來表達相同的意念。Haykin 稱之為「統一的原則」。

統一的原則，可以把相同意念的項目匯聚在同一個標題之下，便利檢索(searching)。如此可以避免相同意念的項目，散見於不同的標題項下。

相同的意念，固然要使用統一的標題，這個原則也可以從寬的適用到意念上大致相同，或大同小異，沒有必要再細分的情況下使用。試舉幾個例子來說明：

1.如果採用了 Ethics 做標題，以下的類似詞語，就不必再選做標題：

Moral philosophy

Moral science

Morality

Morals

Practical ethics

2.Oral medication 選做標題，則下面的詞語就不應再用：

Drugs by mouth

Medication by mouth

3.意念相同，而表達形式不同的情況，譬如採用 Diagnosis, Surgical 則不再採用 Surgical diagnosis，採用 Air--Pollution，而不採用 Air pollution。

然而在某種特殊情況下，卻需要故意重複某些款目(entry)相同，而排列次序(citation order)不同的標題，如：

United States--Foreign relations--France

France--Foreign relation--United States

Haykin 稱之為「重複款目」(duplicate entry)。以上兩個標題款目相同，僅排列的次序不同，其中兩個組成款目，United States 和

France，同樣的重要，並沒有主從的關係。使用者可能從 United States 著手查尋，也可能從 France 著手查尋。在兩個款目同樣重要，相互影響的情況下，重複款目的安排在卡片目標中就有其必要。

其他的例子如：

China--Commerce--Japan

Japan--Commerce--China

重複款目在機讀式目錄系統上已失去其重要性。

三、主題標目的選擇

標題的選擇對整個主題編目制度的良窳有決定性的影響。以英語而言，標題的選擇應該注意下列事項：

1.同義語(synonymous term)

如何在同義語中選擇一個恰當的詞語，作為代表性的標題，Cutter 提供5點原則：

⑴選擇使用者最熟諳的詞語。

⑵其他目錄、索引上最常見的詞語。

⑶在詞義上最明確而不致誤解者。

⑷關鍵字(key word)應在標題的前端。

⑸相關連的主題應盡量的匯集在一起，其方法是使用相同的起首字。

譬如說和教會有關的標題盡量使用 Church 一字做起首語。根據這一原則，教會歷史一詞應採用 Church history，而不用 Ecclesiastical history，如此才能使有關 Church 的標題排列在一起。試看 Church history 和其他有關主題，在 LC Subject Heading 上的排列次序：

Church discipline

Church doors

Church doorways

Church employees

Church entertainments

Church etiquette

Church facilities

Church family

Church finance

Church fund raising

Church furniture

Church gardens

———

Church historians

Church history

———

Church membership

Church music

Church newsletters

2.變體拼音字(variant spelling)的選擇

英語裡許多字有不同的拼法，處理的原則是：

⑴採用當前最流通的拼法，而不用老舊的拼法。

譬如採用 Airplanes，而不用 Aeroplanes。

⑵採用美國英語的拼法。

譬如採用 Labor，而非 Labour；Catalog，而非 Catalogue。

3.美英語和外國語的選擇

美英語系的圖書館，理所當然的應使用英美詞語作標題。然而在有些觀念無法使用適當的英美語表達出來的時候，就有直接使用外來語的必要。譬如：Bonsai, Ch'i kung, Coups d'état。

4.科學術語(scientific term)和常用詞語(popular term)的選擇

對於一個一般性的圖書館而言，應當盡量選擇常用詞語，避免使用科學術語。譬如選擇 Butterflies，而不使用 Lepidoptera diurna，選擇 Horses 而不使用 Equus caballus。至於專門性的圖書館，就必需選擇專門性的科學術語，以便和專門學科書籍上慣用的詞彙配合。如果常用詞語也為專家們所採用，則不妨參酌使用。總之，要以使用者所慣用的詞語做選擇標題的依據。

5.流行詞語(current term)和陳舊詞語(obsolete term)的選擇

毫無疑問的，在原則上，標題應該選擇當前流行的詞語。在實行上卻有困難。

第一層困難是如何察覺到那些詞語已被更新的詞語所取代。語言是一種約定俗成的產物，一個新的事物或觀念初出現的時候，往往有各種不同的名稱，要經過歲月的裁汰，才會產生一個共同接受的詞語。這個過程，可能是短短的幾個月，也可能是漫長的幾年時間。然而圖書編目要在情勢尚未塵埃落定以前，選擇一個詞語做編目之用。這個被採用的詞語，在當初可能是最佳的選擇，到頭來卻可能淪為不流行的詞語。美國國會圖書館在電腦初發明的時候，選擇 Electronic Calculating-machines 做為電腦的標題，曾幾何時 Computers 成為慣用的詞語，取代了 Electronic Calculating-machines。到今天，再使用這個舊名稱，就會使人不知所云了。第二層困難是經常更新標題以維持其流通性，所費不貲。尤其是卡片式的標題制度，一個標題的改動，

往往牽涉到上百成千張的目錄卡片(catalog card)。這是國會圖書館過去數十年來，不輕易做大幅更改的主因。自從電腦取代了卡片，要做大幅度的更改就容易多了。因此從1975年以後，美國國會圖書館標題的更改就比以往頻繁。我們試舉一個例子來做說明。在1987年11月11日，主題編目處把數十年沿用下來的標題 Moving-pictures更換成流行的 Motion pictures。僅僅一個字的更改就波及到593項其他標題及參見(references)的更改。如果是過去卡片式制度的話，還有數以萬計的目錄卡片需要隨著更改。在使用電腦作業的今天，不必動用人工更改每一張卡片。依賴電腦程式(computer program)就可以解決這些棘手的問題。

6.區分同形異義字(homograph)

一個標題，只能代表一個意念，這是主題編目的最基本原則。遇到同形異義字的情況，一定要設法區分出來。最常用的辦法是使用不同結構的詞語來表達不同的意念。

萬一別無他途，非得使用同形字來表達不同的意義，最便捷的辦法是在同形異義字之後，用括弧加上區別的詞語。如：

Cold	Rings (Algebra)
Cold (Disease)	Rings (Gymnastics)

7.款目的直接性(direct entry)

選擇標題時，應選擇和書籍的內容直接相關的標題，不必拐彎抹角地先提到它的類別(class)。譬如說，一本有關貓的書籍，它的標題應該是 Cat，而不是 Domestic animals--Cats。類別是分類法的領域，主題編目應該採用最直截了當的標題來表達書籍的內容。至於應該「直截了當」到什麼程度，這就牽涉到主題標目確切性的問題。

8.款目的確切性(specific entry)

款目的確切性和直接性具有密切的關係，但二者的內涵不應混為一談。後者是指標題應該直接表達書籍的內容，前者是指如何確實地把內容表達出來。

款目的確切性是個相對性而非絕對性的問題。個別標題涵義的廣狹，與這個標題是否確切並沒有關係。真正影響到個別款目確切性的是它使用的場合，也就是說，要判斷一個款目是否確切，必須了解它是使用在什麼場合。我們試就各種不同的場合對主題確切性的影響申述於下：

(1)書籍和款目確切性的關係

每一本書籍的標題是依書籍內容來決定。如果標題（可以是一個標題，也可以是兩個標題以上的組合）著實地涵蓋了一本書的主旨，我們可以說這個（或這組）標題是非常確切的。反過來說，如果標題沒有概括一本書的主旨，或流於過分廣泛，或失之過分狹窄，我們可以說這個（這組）標題不夠確切。我們試舉些例子來說明：

一本有關動物學概論的書，我們使用 Zoology 這一個標題是非常確切的。雖然 Zoology 一詞涵蓋很廣，但對於討論動物學的書籍來說是最恰當不過的。同樣的，一本討論貓的書籍使用 Cats 也屬確切得當，雖然 Cats 一詞的涵蓋要比 Zoology 要狹窄得多。

反過來說，如果使用 Mammals（哺乳動物）一詞於以上兩書，都不確切。對於前者而言 Mammals 一詞不足以包括動物學，對於後者而言，它又顯得太廣泛了。

明瞭了以上的說明，我們對國會圖書館主題編目有關「確切」一詞的定義就很容易了解：「確切性是指標題應該適當的涵蓋一本書的主旨，不多也不少。標題本身的涵義並不能決定它是否確切，我們必需從一本書和它的主題標目之間的關係來決定。譬如說，Economics

這一個涵義很廣泛的標題，對於一本討論經濟學的書本而言是再恰當不過的了。」❻

⑵圖書館制度和主題標目確切性的關係

個別圖書館的性質，庋藏和政策對標題的確切性有密切關係。前面提到過各種圖書館有不同的服務對象，譬如說一個地方公共圖書館它的藏書林林總總，但在每一項專門學科項下的書籍數量往往比大學及專門圖書館少得多。在這個情形之下專門學科的標題就無需劃分得太精細，過於精細的標題往往徒然造成檢索的不便和浪費編目時間。我們試假設一個情況來說明，美國某地方公共圖書館有三、四十本有關中國歷史的圖書，其中有中國通史，也有斷代史，諸如漢史、唐史、宋史以及鴉片戰爭、太平天國之亂、拳亂等書。這個圖書館在將來也不至於大量增加中國歷史方面的書籍，在這個情形下，應該如何確切地表達這些書籍的主旨呢？這裡讓我們先看其他擁有大量中國歷史藏書的圖書館，例如國會圖書館，是如何處置這些書籍的。以下是它所使用的標題：

China--History.

China--History--Han dynasty, 202 B.C–220 A.D.

China--History--T'ang dynasty, 618–907.

China--History--Sung dynasty, 960–1279.

China--History--Opium War, 1840–1842.

China--History--Taiping Rebellion, 1850–1864.

China--History--Boxer Rebellion, 1899–1901.

---

❻ Library of Congress, Subject Cataloging Division, **Regional Institute on Library of Congress Subject Headings: Handbook** (Washington, D.C.: Library of Congress, 1983), pp. 2–8.

如果這個地方公眾圖書館也使用同樣的標題，使僅有的三、四十本書分別隸屬於7種標題，每一個標題之下能有幾本書？主題編目的基本用意是把同性質的書籍集中在同一標題之下，以便查尋。上面的情形卻得到相反的效果，每一項標題之下僅有寥寥幾本書，確切的要求是達到了，但反而造成了檢索的不便和編目時間的浪費。比較實際的編目方法可能是把有關中國歷史的書籍全部安置在一個標題之下，那就是：

China--History

如果這個圖書館的編目部門決定有關中國歷史的書籍在 China--History 之下不再細分，則唐史也罷，太平天國之亂也罷，都將列在 China--History 的標題之下。以這個圖書館的編目原則而言，它的編目方法也算是達到了確切性的目的。

這個例子雖然是假設的，但在實際上，幾乎每一個圖書館都有它們自訂的原則。即以美國國會圖書館而言，它的標題以及分類表的發展，完全是根據館內藏書的多寡而定。藏書量少的學科，其標題和分類表就簡略；藏書量多的學科，其標題和分類表就詳細。再以歷史學科為例。美國歷史在 United States--History 標題下的複分(subdivision)多達四十餘項。（並非全部有關美國歷史的標題皆以 United States--History-- 的形式來表達。在這裡僅舉此一例。）在 China--History 下的複分有九十餘項之多，而許多其他國家歷史下的複分不過寥寥十數項，甚至有不再細分下去的。

前面的敘述，似乎和款目的確切性一節有互相矛盾之處。這裡必須強調的是，主題編目的理想在於利用標題來確切地表達一本書籍的主旨，但在實際作業上，個別圖書館根據情況而制定適合它們環境的編目原則。絕對的確切性可不可能做到，或者說即使能夠做到，對讀

者而言，是不是最有幫助，頗有商榷的餘地。

　　Richard Angell 對確切性作了以下的說明：「標題確切性的程度是取決於一個制度內對某一項目需求多寡而定。」❼

　　9.多層次主題的處理

　　一本書籍如果只有一個主旨，並且能夠使用一個單字(single word)的標題來表達的話是再便捷也不過的了。然而一本書往往具有多層涵義，它們之間的關係可能是主從的，也可能是對等的，用一個單字不足以表達它們之間的關係。在這個情況下就必須使用各種組合的方法來表達這些多層次的涵義。組合的方式大致可以分為下面兩類：

　　⑴預先組合法(precoordination)

　　利用不同的結構法把具有多層次涵義的關係串連起來成為一個標題，這種方法叫「預先組合法」(precoordination)。即在讀者檢索標題之前，主題編目者已經預先把多層次的涵義組合成為一個標題以供檢索。預先組合法有以下數種：

　　①形容詞片語(adjectival phrase)

　　　Criminal liability

　　　Economic forecasting

　　　Electronic measurements

　　　Plant diseases

　　　Plant inspection

　　②連接詞片語(conjunctive phrase)

　　　Church and education

---

❼　Richard S. Angell, *Standards for Subject-Headings: A National Program* (Journal of Cataloging and Classification, Oct. 1954), 10: 193.

Literature and Society

Television and politics

③前置詞片語(prepositional phrase)

Cookery for the sick

Deficiency diseases in plants

Fertilization of plants

Flowers in literature

Pantomimes with music

④單詞或片語限定語(qualifier)

Cookery (Vegetables)

Finite fields (Algebra)

Dove (Transport plane)

Rats (Dog)

⑤單詞或片語加上一個或一個以上的複分

Church architecture--Italy

Physics--Research

Plants--Identification

Railroads--France--History--19th Century--Pictorial works

Great Britain--Kings and rulers--Journeys--Canada--Juvenile literature

⑥以上數種的組合

Church and labor-Italy

Choruses, Secular (Unison) with instrumental ensemble

Clocks and watches in art

Piano, trumpet, viola with orchestra-scores

這幾種結構，將在第五章加以說明。

⑵自行組合法(postcoordination)

第二種方法是將多層次的涵義一一列出，成為幾個各別的標題，並不過問它們之間的關係，而讓檢索者在這些標題之間自行組合，這種方法叫「自行組合法」(postcoordination)。自行組合法通常用在涵義複雜的書籍，它們之間的關係很難預為組合成一個合理的標題來表達整體的關係。目前國會圖書館的主題編目法大部分是採取「預先組合法」，以下是一個實際的例子 ❽：

書名：*The tariff on sugar in the United States.*

過去使用「自行組合法」，所用的標題是：

1. Sugar trade––United States.

2. Tariff––United States.

現在使用「預先組合法」所用的標題是：

1. Tariff on sugar––United States.

雖然國會圖書館主題編目趨向「預先組合法」，有不少情況仍然需要使用「自行組合法」。譬如：

書名：*Crocheting Novelty Potholders*

1. Crocheting.

2. Potholders.

書名：*Iron Deficiency in Women*

1. Iron deficiency diseases.

2. Women––Diseases.

❽ 同❻，pp. 2–10。

第五章　主題標目的結構

美國國會圖書館的標題是由各種不同形式的詞語及符號組合而成。

在這一章裡我們將介紹國會圖書館現有主標題(main heading)的結構。主標題之後的複分(subdivision)留待第六章討論。

編目作業可以劃分為兩大類別：著錄編目與主題編目。前者的主要工具書是美國國會圖書館協會(American Library Association)出版的 "*Anglo-American Cataloguing Rules*"。目前最新的版本是1998年改訂的第二版。

本書專職於主題編目，所以凡是屬於著錄編目範圍的標題，譬如：人名、行政地區名稱、書籍、刊物名稱、公司行號以及機關團體名稱，皆不在本書討論範圍之內。

主題編目的主要工具書是美國國會圖書館出版的兩部工具書：

1. 《國會圖書館主題標目表》(*Library of Congress Subject Headings*)

每年出版一次，最新版本是1999年的第二十二版。

2. 《主題編目手冊》(*Subject Cataloging Manual: Subject Headings*)

最新的版本是1998年修訂的第五版。

這是主題編目的最主要兩部工具書，研究及使用國會圖書館主題編目者，不可不備。

國會圖書館常用的主標題主要可以歸納成以下6種形式 ❶：（屬於主題編目範疇的自然地理標題有其特定的組成規章，不在此討論。）

一、單字標題

這是最簡單的一種形式：一個標題由一個單字組成，表達一項完整的意義。如：

Democracy

Gravity

Kidneys

Psychology

Topology

Weeds

二、形容詞片語標題

這是由名詞加上它的形容詞組成的標題。如：

Chinese poetry

Automobile supplies industry

Election law

Ocean currents

Fawcett family

---

❶ Lois Mai Chan, *Library of Congress Subject Headings: Principles and Applications*, 3rd. ed. (Littleton, Colorado: Libraries Unlimited, 1995), pp. 43–53.

Submarine warfare

Electric rocket engines

Student teachers

Women's rights

Rotating amplifiers

Paralytic shellfish poisoning

三、連接詞片語標題

這是由連接詞 and, or 組合而成的標題。如:

Stores or stock-room keeping

Christianity and culture

College and school drama

Restitution and indemnification claims

Sugar laws and legislation

Command and control systems

連接詞片語的使用通常限於下列情況:

1.兩個（或兩個以上）經常相提並論的概念，或者它們之間的概念非常接近，不必再細分成單獨的標題。如:

Good and evil

Books and reading

Encyclopedias and dictionaries

Courts and courtiers

Emigration and immigration

Automobile wrecking and used parts industry

2.表示兩個相互影響的概念。如:

Authors and readers

Crops and climate

Agriculture and energy

Literature and society

Technology and civilization

Drinking and traffic accidents

Women and the military

Education and crime

Government and the press

Television and reading

四、前置詞片語標題

Anesthesia in neurology

Baseball for children

Frequencies of oscillating systems

Judgments by default

Law of large numbers

Oil pollution of the sea

Timpani with orchestra

Frontier and pioneer life in art

五、外加限定語標題

限定語可以是單字，也可以是片語。它們通常以括弧的形式附加在標題之後。它們的作用是：

1.區分同形異義語。如：

Creation

Creation (Islam)

Creation (Literary, artistic, etc.)

Forms (Mathematics)

Forms (Roman law)

2.補註詞義不明的詞彙或外來語。如：

Gab (Artificial language)

Line play (Football)

Fon (African people)

Sandy (Dog)

Ch'i (Chinese philosophy)

Chhau (Dance)

CHOICES (Information retrieval system)

3.限定一個標題的範圍。如：

Oaths (Jewish law)

Change (Psychology)

Cookery (Chicken)

Coaching (Athletics)

Legalism (Chinese philosophy)

六、倒置標題

倒置標題(inverted heading)的作用是把最重要的詞語，通常是名詞，反其自然的字順(natural order of words)，排置於標題的最前端(initial position)。英語片語的組成通常是形容詞語在被形容詞語的前面，關鍵字是被形容的詞語。如果按照自然的英文字順來編排標題，關鍵字在標題的順序上顯得無足輕重，次要的形容詞語反而居排列的首位。有鑑於此，才有倒置標題的辦法。如：

Animals, Mythical

Architecture, Tudor

Archives, Technical

Chaplains, Military

Chemistry, Analytic

Judgments, Criminal

Maps, Pictorial

Numbers, Complex

倒置標題的原來用意固佳，但是當今大部分的圖書館在電腦取代了卡片之後，倒置標題對檢索的影響就有重新審視的必要。新式的電腦，以國會圖書館的電腦為例，標題的檢索可以從標題中任何一個字開始，不必呆板的依標題字的排列順序來索求。舉例來說，以 Animals, Mythical 或以 Mythical animals 在電腦上從事檢索，其所得的結果是一樣的，也就是說關鍵字是不是居於標題的前端並不重要。準此，為達到標題一致性的要求，將來標題的編製可以不必倒置其詞語，而完全以英語詞語的自然順序來製作標題。有鑑於此，國會圖書

館在1992年以後，逐漸地將倒置標題修改成依自然順序的標題。

譬如 Libraries, Naval; Libraries, Catholic，都改成了 Naval libraries, Catholic libraries。然而目前還存在許多倒置標題。

以上6種形式的主標題加上主標題之後的複分，一共有7種不同的形式可以用來組織標題。而一個主題往往可以使用不同的形式來表達，究竟在什麼情形之下應該選擇什麼形式來組成標題呢？這是從事編目工作者經常提出的問題，不幸它也是非常棘手的一個問題。

主題編目單位過去沒有一個明確的規範(code)來統籌標題的製作，長年下來標題的製作就呈現出許多矛盾不一致的現象。究其原因不外以下幾個因素：

1.從1898年國會圖書館主題標目表開始編纂以來，標題的製作是視館內藏書的需要而訂定，也就是說它的標題完全反映館內的藏書。館內沒有收藏的學科，其標題也就付諸闕如。因此，標題每有不周全或不平衡的現象。

2.現存的標題是漫長歲月累積的結果，其間經過無數人事的更替，思想的變遷，以及詞彙的消長，難免有矛盾或不合時宜之處。現存的標題與其說是反映當今最新主題標目理論的成果，毋寧說是標題遞嬗演變的歷程。

3.以編目處有限的人力物力，它無法隨時刪除更改不合時宜以及不合現今編目規則的標題。

以上諸般問題是國會圖書館主題編目受到外界詬病最多的地方。然而批評者雖眾，能夠提出全盤改革方案者卻絕無僅有。從過去的著述及經驗上，我們歸納出幾項概念性的原則於下：

1.以簡單明確為基本原則。Cutter 認為凡是能夠用單字表達的標題，就選用單字而不用片語。譬如說不用 Moral philosophy 而用

Ethics做標題；不用 Mental philosophy 而用 Intellect或 Mind ❷。

　　2.在不同形式的片語中選擇一個做標題時，Cutter 認為，要硬性製定一個規範來統籌片語的選擇是不可能的，唯一的辦法是選擇最常用的片語來作標題 ❸。

　　3.在一個主題內的其他意念盡量使用複分的辦法來表達，而不用片語。除非那個片語是大家所常用者。目前國會圖書館的標題製作正朝這個原則做修訂。如 ❹：

修訂前的標題	修訂後的標題
Social science research	Social sciences--Research
Color of flowers	Flowers--Color
Teachers, rating of	Teachers--Rating of

---

❷　Charles A. Cutter, *Rules for a Dictionary Catalog*, 4th. ed. (Washington, D.C.: Government Printing Office, 1904), p. 72.

❸　同❷, p. 74。

❹　同❶, p. 49。

第六章　主題標目的複分

國會圖書館編目處使用"--"的符號把主標題(main heading)再細分下去，成為一組串連的標題。這種在主標題之後再細分下去的項目，稱為複分(subdivision)。

複分的作用有二：一是使得標題更具確切性；二是把數量太多的主標題劃分成較小的單位，便利檢索。

國會圖書館標題的複分可以依它們的性質區分為4種：

內容複分(topical subdivision)

地區複分(geographic subdivision)

年代複分(chronological subdivision)

形式複分(form subdivision)

內容複分在機讀式目錄 MARC(Machine Readable Catalog的簡稱)的代號是"X"，地區複分的代號是"Z"，年代複分的代號是"Y"，形式複分的代號是"V"。（1999年以前形式複分的代號與內容複分沒有區別，也是"X"。1999年以後採用"V"做代號，以別於內容複分。）

茲將這4種複分敘述於下。

一、內容複分

內容複分用在主標題之後以限制、縮小主標題的涵義及範圍。如：

Automobiles--Air Conditioning.

Blood--Circulation.

Cattle--Anatomy.

Chinese Chess--End games.

複分之後還允許再複分。譬如:

Buddhism--Doctrines--History.

Brain--Diseases--Diagnosis.

Airplanes--Motors--Carburetors.

Automobiles--Defects--Law and legislation--United States.

Mathematics--Study and teaching--Japan--Audio-visual aids.

《國會圖書館主題標目》(*Library of Congress Subject Headings*,簡稱 LCSH) 在每一個主標題之下列出可以使用在此項主標題後的複分。這些複分是經過擬議,然後得到使用授權(authorized)的複分,編目者不得擅自使用沒有獲得授權(non-authorized)的複分。唯一的例外是通用複分(free-floating subdivision),它們雖然沒有列在主標題之下,卻可視情況而使用。我們將在本章的最後一節再討論通用複分。

二、地區複分

如果一本書籍的內容(topic)具有地區性,那麼代表這本書的主標題就應有地區複分。

在1976年12月以前國會圖書館主題編目的地區複分有兩種辦法:第一種辦法是直接地區複分(direct local subdivision),即在主標題之後直接加上地區的名稱。不論這個地區的行政區劃是省,州,縣、市或

鄉鎮都可以直接加在主標題之後。如：

Art--Paris.

Banks and banking--Shanghai.

Education--Bavaria.

Farm corporations--Kwangtung, China (Province)

Bank loans--Pusan, Korea.

Gas industry--Ibaraki (Prefecture)

Finance--Manchuria.

這種直接地區複分在1976年12月以後已為間接地區複分(indirect local subdivision)所取代 ❶。

　　第二種辦法即是間接地區複分。以下是間接地區複分的例子，讀者可以比較它與直接地區複分不同之處：

Art--France--Paris.

Banks and banking--China--Shanghai.

Education--Germany--Bavaria.

Farm corporations--China--Kwangtung Province.

Bank loans--Korea--Pusan.

Gas industry--Japan--Ibaraki--Ken.

Finance--China--Manchuria.

　　間接地區複分的基本規則是 ❷：

---

❶ Library of Congress, *Subject Cataloging Manual: Subject Headings*, 5 th. ed. (Washington, D.C.: Library of Congress, 1996), H830, p. 1.

❷ Library of Congress, Subject Cataloging Division, *Library of Congress Subject Headings; A Guide to Subdivision Practice* (Washington, D. C.: Library of Congress, 1981), pp. 3–4.

1.任何主標題或內容複分之後如果沒有可以使用地區複分的符號 (May Subd Geog)不得使用地區複分。

間接地區複分過去使用的符號是 (Indirect)，現在為 (May Subd Geog) 所取代，它是 May Subdivide Geographically 的簡稱。

2.地區複分的符號出現在主標題之後時，如：Construction industry (May Subd Geog)表示這個主標題之後可以有地區複分，如：Construction industry--Poland。如果還需要其他的複分，譬如內容或形式複分時，這些複分應置於地區複分之後，如：Construction industry--Poland--Finance。這種在主標題之後的地區複分是最常見的一種。此外還有兩種例外的情況：

⑴地區複分使用在內容複分之後。

⑵地區複分同時使用在主標題及內容複分之後。

這兩種例外情況將在後面再加討論。

3.如果要複分的地區是在一個國家的行政區劃之內，這個地區的複分一定要先通過這個地區所屬的國家名稱，成為雙層次的地區複分。也就是：

〔主標題〕--〔國家〕--〔地區〕

例如：

Banks and banking--China--Shanghai.

Housing--China--Kwangtung Province.

Painting--France--Paris.

Education--Japan--Saitama--Ken.

Industrial management--Italy--Milan.

這裡所謂的「地區」，可以解釋為：

⑴一個國家之內的任何現行行政區劃，它可以是省、縣、市、鄉

鎮、村、區等，視每一個國家的行政區劃而有所不同。

　　(2)它可以是一個國家歷史上的行政區劃或單位。例如：

　　　　Taxation--Spain--Leon (Kingdom)

　　　　Elephants--Tunisia--Carthage (Ancient city)

　　(3)它可以是一個國家內的自然地理名稱。如山、湖、河流、島嶼、峽谷等。例如：

　　　　Agriculture--China--Yangtzu River Valley.

　　　　Archaeologists--Greece--Aegina Island.

　　　　Plant breeding--Ethiopia--Simen Mountains Region.

　　(4)如果要複分的地區是國家或大於國家的地域(region)，或分屬於兩個（或兩個以上）國家，這些地區就可以直接複分在主標題之後，成為單層次的地區複分。即：

　　　　〔主標題〕--〔國家〕

　　　　〔主標題〕--〔大於國家的地區〕

　　　　〔主標題〕--〔分屬兩個國家（或兩個以上）的地區〕

例如：

　　　　Religion, Prehistoric--India.

　　　　Agriculture--Black Sea Region.

　　　　Mountains--East Asia.

　　上述兩種基本規則有幾項例外，它們是：

　　(1)三個特定的國家，美國(United States)、加拿大(Canada)、英國(Great Britain)在間接地區複分時第一個層次並非國家。它們在間接地區複分的第一個行政層次是：

　　美國以州(state)為第一層次，加拿大以省(province)為第一層次，英國以其四個組成單元為第一層次 ❸：

美國：

Alabama

Alaska

Arizona

Arkansas

California

Colorado

Connecticut

Delaware

Florida

Georgia

Hawaii

Idaho

Illinois

Indiana

Iowa

Kansas

Kentucky

Louisiana

Maine

Maryland

Massachusetts

Michigan

Minnesota

---

❸ 同❶，H830, p. 5。

Mississippi

Missouri

Montana

Nebraska

Nevada

New Hampshire

New Jersey

New Mexico

New York (State)

North Carolina

North Dakota

Ohio

Oklahoma

Oregon

Pennsylvania

Rhode Island

South Carolina

South Dakota

Tennessee

Texas

Utah

Vermont

Virginia

Washington (State)

West Virginia

Wisconsin

Wyoming

加拿大：

Alberta

British Columbia

Manitoba

New Brunswick

Newfoundland

Northwest Territories

Nova Scotia

Ontario

Prince Edward Island

Québec (Province)

Saskatchewan

Yukon Territory

英國：

England

Northern Ireland

Scotland

Wales

例如：

Education--California--San Joaquin Valley.

Tourism--California--San Francisco.

Music--Ontario--Toronto.

Sports--England--London Metropolitan Area.

如果所要複分的地區大於州、省，或組成單元時，這些地區就必須直接複分在主標題之後，而不必通過上述的行政層次。如：

Zoology--Northwest, Pacific.

Geology--Rocky Mountains.

Fishes--Saint Lawrence River.

Education--Southern States.

Saint Lawrence River 屬加拿大，Rocky Mountains, Southern States, 和 Northwest, Pacific 屬美國，它們皆大於省州的層次。

(2)一個國家的區域，如果它所組成的標題是〔國家〕，＋〔區域〕的形式，這種標題在地區複分時即直接複分在主標題之後，成為單層次的地區複分。例如：

Geology--China, Northwest.

Geology--Brazil, Northeast.

Nutrition surveys--Italy, Southern.

對於以上三國而言，如果它所組成的標題是〔州、省、或組成單位〕，＋〔區域〕的形式，這種標題也直接複分在主標題之後，成為單層次的地區複分。例如：

Geology--California, Southern.

(3)二個特定的城市(city)直接複分於主標題之後，而不必通過其他行政層次。它們是華盛頓特區(Washington, D.C.)，以及耶路撒冷(Jerusalem)。例如：

Taxation--Washington (D.C.)

Hospitals--Jerusalem.

(4)島嶼的特殊處置辦法

①如果島嶼或群島遠離大陸，採取直接複分，即使這些島嶼並非

獨立的政治體，如：

> Geology--Bermuda Islands.

②如果島嶼或群島離大陸不遠，並且是屬於一個國家的行政體制時，採取間接複分。如：

> Agriculture--Italy--Sicily.

③對於群島中的一個島嶼，它的複分是間接通過群島的層次。如：

> Water--supply--Canary Islands--Teneriffe.

(5)間接地區複分的符號也可以出現在內容複分之後。如：

> History--Study and teaching (May Subd Geog)

這表示內容複分之後可以有地區複分。如：

> History--Study and teaching--Singapore.

主標題 History 之後沒有 May Subd Geog 的記號，不能有地區複分。

(6)間接地區複分的符號也可以同時出現在主標題及內容複分之後。如：

> Construction industry (May Subd Geog)--
>
> Law and legislation (May Subd Geog)

在這個情形下地區複分應置於內容複分之後。如：

> Construction industry--Law and legislation--Poland--Warsaw.

也就是說，後面的地區複分記號自動取代前面的地區複分記號。這種在內容複分之後允許有地區複分的情況，只限於少數特定的內容複分。

三、年代複分

年代複分用在主標題之後，以劃分主標題所代表的特定年代。年代的選擇是依據每一個主標題的需要而特別擬定的。這些擬定的年代通常代表個別主標題歷史發展及演變的重要過程。如：

Philosophy, Chinese--To 221 B.C.

Japan--History--Meiji period, 1868-1912.

English literature--Early modern, 1500-1700.

Music--Theory--500-1400.

North Carolina--History--Civil War, 1861-1865.

Theater--History--Medieval, 500-1500.

Painting, Japanese--Edo period, 1600-1868.

Church history--Middle Ages, 600-1500.

Great Britain--Civilization--1066-1485.

France--Politics and government--1715-1774.

另外一種年代複分是為了避免主標題的數量過於龐大而設計的。這一類的年代複分並沒有什麼真正的時代意義，它們的存在只是為了方便檢索而已。如：

World politics--1955-1965.

　　　　　　--1965-1975.

　　　　　　--1975-1985.

另一種是以書籍出版的時期為年代複分的依據。如：

Mathematics--Early works to 1800.

Education--Early works to 1800.

四、形式複分

　　形式複分是用來說明書籍的類型。譬如字典、期刊、索引、目錄等等。它們和書籍的內容無關。這一種複分也屬於通用複分。在標題的組合中，形式複分通常是居於整個標題的末端。譬如：

　　China--History--Ch'ing dynasty, 1644–1912--Bibliography

　　Chemistry, Analytic--Abstracts

　　Hydrology--Periodicals

　　Population--Statistics

五、通用複分

　　除了以上所討論的4種複分外，還有一種重要的複分，即所謂的通用複分(free-floating subdivision)。

　　任何一個主標題之後的複分都必須在使用之前由編目者擬議(proposal)，經主題編審會議通過之後才能使用，其過程相當費時。複分的擬議通常是為了某一個特殊的複分使用在某一個特定的主標題之下而提出的。然而有許多複分可以廣泛的運用在許多主標題之下，譬如說：形式複分"Dictionaries"幾乎可能使用在任何一個主題之下，諸如Chinese literature--Dictionaries; Political science--Dictionaries; Plants--Dictionaries; Chemical engineering--Dictionaries; Accounting--Dictionaries。如果逐一擬議待審核通過後再使用，實不勝其煩。為了簡化內容及形式複分的使用過程，編目處乃製訂了一系列最常用的複分，訂定它們的定義和使用範圍註釋(scope note)。只要在符合使用範

圍的情況下，這些複分可以自由的應用在所需的主標題之下。通用複分就是基於這種實際的需要而產生的，要言之，通用複分是內容及形式複分的局部使用自由化，它本身並非複分的一種，而是複分的應用。

通用複分依它們使用的場合分成5大類：

1.用在模範標題下的通用複分(Free-flooting subdivisions controlled by pattern headings)

在同類型的主標題中挑選一項，列出所有適用的複分作為其他同類型主標題的模範或樣本。譬如說，文學類型的複分是以英國文學(English literature)為模範，任何其他國家的文學皆以英國文學下的複分為通用複分。以下共列46項模範標題，我們可以依它們的類別分列於下❹：

主　　題	類　　別	模範標題
Subject Field	*Category*	*Pattern Heading(s)*
RELIGION	Religious and monastic orders	Jesuits
	Religions	Buddhism
	Christian denominations	Catholic Church
	Sacred works (including parts)	Bible

---

❹ Library of Congress, *Subject Cataloging Manual: Subject Headings*, 5 th. ed, (Washington, D.C.: Library of Congress, 1996), H.1146, pp. 4–6.

主　題	類　別	模範標題
Subject Field	*Category*	*Pattern Heading(s)*
HISTORY GEOGRAPHY	Colonies of individual countries	Great Britain–Colonies
	Legislative bodies (including individual chambers)	United States. Congress
	Military services (including armies, navies, marines, etc.)	United States–Armed Forces
		United States. Air Force
		United States. Army
		United States. Marine Corps
		United States. Navy
	Wars	World War, 1939–1945
		United States–History–Civil War, 1861–1865

主　題	類　別	模範標題
Subject Field	*Category*	*Pattern Heading(s)*
SOCIAL SCIENCES	Industries	Construction industry
		Retail trade
	Types of educational institutions	Universities and colleges
	Individual educational institutions	Harvard University
	Legal topics	Labor laws and legislation

主　題	類　別	模範標題
Subject Field	*Category*	*Pattern Heading(s)*
THE ARTS	Group of literary authors (including authors, poets, dramatists, etc.)	Auhtors, English
	Literary works entered under author	Shakespeare, William, 1564-1616. Hamlet
	Literary works entered under title	Beowulf
	Languages and groups of languages	English language French language Romance languages
	Literatures (including individual genres)	English literature
	Musical compositions	Operas
	Musical instruments	Piano

主　題	類　別	模範標題
Subject Field	*Category*	*Pattern Heading(s)*
SCIENCE AND TECHNOLOGY	Land vehicles	Automobiles
	Materials	Concrete Metals
	Chemicals	Copper Insulin
	Organs and regions of the body	Heart Foot
	Diseases	Cancer Tuberculosis
	Plants and crops	Corn
	Animals	Fishes Cattle

以下是46項模範標題的實例:

Fishes--Eggs--Incubation

Cattle--Diseases (May Subd Geog)

Copper--Metallography

Great Britain--Colonies--Administration

Cancer--Radiotherapy (May Subd Geog)

Tuberculosis--Prognosis

Harvard University--Degrees

Universities and colleges--Entrance requirements

Indians of North America--Population

Construction industry--Cost control

Retail trade--Security measures

English language--Syntax

French language--Dialects

Romance languages--Classification

Labor laws and legislation--Criminal provisions

United States Congress--Committees

Authors, English--Correspondence

Shakespeare, William, 1564-1616--Museums

Shakespeare, William, 1564-1616. Hamlet

Beowulf--Adaptations

English literature--Foreign influences

Concrete--Finishing

Metals--Carbon content

United States--Armed Forces--Civilian employees

United States. Air Force--Aviation mechanics

United States. Army--Artillery--Drill and tactics

United States. Marine Corps--Aviation

United States. Navy--Signalmen

Operas--Characters

Piano--Performance

Wagner, Richard, 1813–1883--Homes and haunts

Newspapers--Local editions

Heart--Blood--vessels

Foot--Abnormalities

Corn--Breeding

Jesuits--Missions

Buddhism--Rituals

Catholic Church--Clergy

Lincoln, Abraham, 1809–1865--Medals

Napoleon I, Emperor of the French, 1769–1821--Will

Bible--Chronology

Soccer--Rules

Salvation--Sermons

Automobiles--Luberication

World War, 1939–1945--Refugees

United States--History--Civil War, 1861–1865--Propaganda.

至於這常用模範標題下的個別通用複分請見附錄一。

　　2.用在地區名稱之下的通用複分(Free-floating subdivisions un-der name of places) 請見附錄二。

　　3.用在水源之下的複分(Free-floating subdivisions under bodies of water)，請見附錄三。

　　4.用在個人(person)、機關(corporate body)、以及種族(ethnic

group)名稱之下的複分。它們的複分細表請見附錄四，五，六。

　5.用在職業類別(classes of persons)之下的複分。它的複分細表請見附錄七。

　6.一般通用的形式及內容複分(commonly used forms and topical subdivisions)。

　除了上面四種使用在特別場所以外的通用複分，還有一種一般通用複分，不限特別場所，應用廣泛，凡適當場所皆可應用，這些一般通用複分限於內容及形式複分，它們的細表請見附錄八。

　1989年後，國會圖書館每年出版一本《複分索引》(*Free-Floating Subdivisions: An Alphabetical Index*)，把分散在各表項內成千的各種複分綜合成一表，按字母順序排列，以便參照。

六、其他通用詞語

　除了以上所介紹的幾種複分之外，還有兩種情況具有「通用」的功能，可以一併於此介紹。

　1.衍生複分(multiple subdivision)

　衍生複分是把複分的某一字加上方形括弧(bracket)，即〔　〕，用來表示這一個字可使用其他同種類的字來替代，而不必逐一擬議。這些衍生複分字所依附的複分本身可能已經是通用複分的一部分，再允許其中的某一個字自由的替代，更進一步增強通用複分的功能❺。例如：

　　World war, 1939–1945--Personal narratives, American, 〔French, German, etc.〕

---

❺ 同❶，H1090, pp. 1-4。

Abortion--Religious aspects--Buddhism〔Christianity, etc.〕

Names, Personal—Scottish,〔Spanish, Welsh, etc.〕

〔地名〕--History--Siege,〔date〕

2. 通用詞語(free-floating terms and phrases)

它和前面所討論的通用複分不同之處是它並非複分而是主標題結構的一部分。在這一章裡討論不屬於複分的標題，似有不對題之弊，然而它的「通用」性質與功能卻和通用複分極為相似，在這裡一併提出討論比較容易了解。

通用詞語的作用和通用複分一樣，是將主標題的某一部分通用化，俾便自由使用。通用詞語目前並沒有廣泛的採用，它們只用在下列數項❻：

(1)〔都市名〕Metropolitan Area

例如:

Atlanta Metropolitan Area (Ga.)

Salt Lake City Metropolitan Area (Utah)

(2)〔都市名〕Region

例如:

Dallas Region (Tex.)

Shanghai Region (China)

(3)〔都市名〕Suburban Area

例如:

Beijing Suburban Area (China)

Atlanta Suburban Area (Ga.)

(4)〔地區名〕Region

---

❻　同❶，H362，pp. 1-3。

例如：

　　Red Sea Region

　　Tai Mountains Region (China)

⑸〔河流名稱〕Region

例如：

　　Potomac River Region

　　Tweed River Region (Scotland and England)

七、複分的順序

複分有兩種基本的順序，即為：

1.〔地區〕--〔內容複分〕

2.〔主題〕--〔地區複分〕

先談第一種。第一種通常是以地方、國家或河流為主題，而以內容為複分。有關這類複分，請參見附錄二，三。

這類複分可以延伸為以下的複分順序：

　　〔地區〕--〔內容複分〕--〔年代複分〕--〔形式複分〕

例如：

　　United States--Social conditions--1980 --Bibliography.

　　China--Civilization--1644--1912--Dictionaries.

第二種通常是以主題為主，而其本身在主題標目表內又可以再允許地區複分，即〔主題〕(May Subd Geog)

這類複分可以延伸為以下的兩種複分順序：

1.〔主題〕--〔地區複分〕--〔內容複分〕--〔年代複分〕--〔形式複分〕

例如:

Railroads--France--Cars--History--19th century--Pictorial works--Juvenile literature.

以上的例子有兩個形式複分。

--Pictorial works

--Junenile literature

我們在前面提過形式複分通常是居於其他複分之後。但是形式複分之後，往往可以再接上另一個形式複分。這並不違反形式複分是在其他複分之後的原則。

2.〔主題〕--〔內容複分〕--〔地區複分〕--〔年代複分〕--〔形式複分〕

例如:

Tuberculosis--Patients--Hospital care--Maryland--Baltimore--History --20th century--Bibliography.

第七章　主題的分析和主題標目的選擇

　　主題編目的終極目的是提供檢索者一個方便的工具，以期在最短的時間內找到他們需要的書籍。如果檢索者對某一特定主題感興趣，希望從浩瀚的書海中找到適當的書籍，最快捷的途徑是從標題著手。標題的重要性實毋庸置疑。

　　本章所要討論的是如何分析書籍的內容，俾使其歸納於適當的標題之下，以供檢索。

一、主題的分析

　　1.款目的確切性　確切性是主題編目的基本原則，我們已在第四章中討論過，不在此重複。以下提供更多的例子，以供參考 ❶ 。

　　⑴書名: **Cats**

　　　標題: Cats.

　　⑵書名: **Siamese cats**

　　　標題: Siamese cat.

---

❶ Library of Congress, Subject Cataloging Division, **Regional Institute on Library of Congress Subject Headings: Handbook** (Washington, D. C.: Library of Congress, 1983), pp. 2–8.

⑶書名：*Canadian tax credit systems: an introductory bibliography*

標題：Tax Credits--Canada--Bibliography.

⑷書名：*Targeted jobs tax credit*

標題：New jobs tax credit--United States.

⑸書名：*Automatic transmission*

標題：Automobiles--Transmission devices, Automatic.

⑹書名：*Death education: a concern for the living*

標題：Death--Study and teaching--United States.

2.對一本書做全盤性的瞭解而將其全書主旨以確切的標題表示出來。切忌單獨對每一篇章作分析而分別提供反映每一篇章的主題，除非那一本書在主旨之外又另外特別強調某些論題，而這些論題通常並不包涵在主旨之內，它的篇幅又佔全書百分之二十以上❷。（百分之二十的規定並無任何特殊依據，只是一個概略性的編目原則，以便編目者能有所遵循。）

⑴書名：*Beginning gymnastics*

標題：Gymnastics.

⑵書名：*Renovascular hypertension*

標題：Renal hypertension.

⑶書名：*Picardie: cadre naturel, histoire, littérature, langue, économie, traditions populaires*

標題：Picardy (France)

⑷書名：*The Great political theories: From Plato and Aris-*

---

❷ Library of Congress, *Subject Cataloging Manual: Subject Headings*, (Washington, D.C.: Library of Congress, 1998), H180, pp. 2–5.

totle to Locke and Montesquieu, from Burke,
Rousseau, and Kant to modern times

標題： Political science. （不必把每一個人名當做標題）

(5)書名： ***Animals*** （其中有一半的分量是討論 camels）

標題： 1. Animals.

2. Camels.

(6)書名： ***A history of Europe, with chapters on Turkey and***
Iran

標題： 1. Europe--History.

2. Turkey--History.

3. Iran--History.

（Turkey 和 Iran 並不屬於 Europe，而這兩項論題各佔20％左右的篇幅。）

二、主題標目的選擇

1. 一個主題　一本書如果全然討論一個主題，只需要提供一個相關的標題。要強調的是一個相關的標題有時可能是一組包括兩個以上的標題，視規章而有所不同。

(1)書名： ***Beyond burnout***

標題： Burn-out (Psychology)

(2)書名： ***Introduction to modern microeconomics***

標題： Microeconomics.

(3)書名： ***Goethe's Italian journey***

標題： 1. Goethe, Johann Wolfgang von, 1749–1832--Journeys-

　　－Italy.

　　2. Italy––Description and travel.

　　3. Authors, German––18th century––Journeys––Italy.

這一組標題是根據處理傳記的規章而製訂的。

　2.兩個主題　一本書如果有兩個主題，而確定並沒有任何一個（或一組）標題可以同時代表這兩個主題，則分別提供代表這兩個主題的標題。

⑴書名：*Handbook of space astronomy and astrophysics*

　標題：　1. Astronomy––Handbooks, manuals, etc.

　　　　　2. Astrophysics––Handbooks, manuals, etc.

⑵書名：*Plate tectonics and crustal evolution*

　標題：　1. Earth––Crust.

　　　　　2. Plate tectonics.

　3.三個主題　一本書如果有三個主題，而確定並沒有任何一個（或一組）標題可以同時代表這三個主題，則分別提供代表這三個主題的標題。

⑴書名：*Ireland––land, politics, and people*

　標題：　1. Land tenure––Ireland––History.

　　　　　2. Ireland––Politics and government.

　　　　　3. Social classes––Ireland––History.

⑵書名：*Easy-to-make wooden candlesticks, chandeliers, and lamps*

　標題：　1. Lamps.

　　　　　2. Chandeliers.

　　　　　3. Candlesticks.

　　4. Woodwork.

(3)書名: ***Tennessee's presidents***

　　標題:　1. Presidents--United States--Biography.

　　　　　2. Jackson, Andrew, 1767-1845.

　　　　　3. Polk, James K. (James Knox), 1795-1849.

　　　　　4. Johnson, Andrew, 1808-1875.

　　　　　5. Tennessee--Biography.

這一組標題是根據處理傳記的規章而製訂的。

　　4. 如果一本書的主題超過三項, 而沒有一個 (或一組) 恰當的標題來代表這些主題時, 則應使用一個較廣泛的標題來代表這些主題, 即使這個標題的範圍超越了那本書的範圍。

　　書名: ***The middle passage: impressions of five societies-- British, French, and Dutch--in the West Indies and South America***

　　標題:　Caribbean Area--Description and travel.

(Caribbean Area 的範圍大於書的範圍)

　　5. 一本書籍如果有地區性, 所有的標題都應有表示這個地區的標題或複分。如:

　　書名: ***America's waste: managing for risk***

　　標題:　1. Refuse and refuse disposal--United States.

　　　　　2. Factory and trade waste--Environmental aspects-- United States.

　　　　　3. Environmental policy--United States.

　　　　　4. Environmental protection--United States.

　　6. 一本書如果全部或部分是特別的類型, 如期刊、目錄、索引

等，應使用形式複分把它的類型在標題上表示出來。如：

書名： *Delaware occupational employment statistics*

標題： 1. Labor supply--Delaware--Statistics.

2. Employment--Delaware--Statistics.

7.兼顧作者或出版者對書籍的意旨。有些書籍是為了特定的對象而寫的，有些是為了特別的形式而寫的，編目者在製訂標題時應在主題之外，兼顧這些意旨。如：

書名： *A textbook of psychology for nurses*

標題： 1. Psychology.

2. Nursing--Psychology aspects.

書名： *Where the wild horses roam* （兒童讀物）

標題： Wild horses--United States--Juvenile literature.

8.如果一本書所代表的主題是主題標目表中沒有的，主題編目者即應依照《主題編目手冊：主題標目》的規定來擬設新的標題。

以下是國會圖書館主題標目應用的實例：

人文學 (HUMANITIES):

書名： *Pearls in the shell: best loved short verses from the Chinese language*

標題： Chinese poetry--Translations into English.

書名： *Studies on the Han fu*

標題： 1. Fu--History and criticism.

2. Chinese poetry--Ch'in and Han dynasties, 221 B.C.-220 A.D. --History and criticism.

書名： *Immortals, festivals, and poetry in medieval China:*

studies in social and intellectual history

標題： 1. Chinese poetry--History and criticism.

2. Religion in poetry.

3. Festivals--China.

4. China--Religious life and customs.

書名： *Taiwan literature, English translation series = T'ai-wan wen hsueh Ying i ts'ung k'an*

標題： 1. Chinese literature--20th century--Translations into English--Periodicals.

2. Chinese literature--Taiwan--Periodicals.

書名： *A dream of red mansions = [Hung lou meng]: saga of a noble Chinese family*

標題： 1. Ts'ao, Hsueh-Ch'in, ca. 1717–1763--Fiction.

2. China--History--Ch'ing dynasty, 1644–1912--Fiction.

書名： *Rereading the stone: desire and the making of fiction in Dream of the red chamber*

標題： 1. Ts'ao, Hsueh-ch'in, ca. 1717–1763. Hung lou meng.

2. Chinese fiction--History and criticism.

書名： *The story of stone: intertextuality, ancient Chinese stone lore, and the stone symbolism in Dream of the red chamber, Water margin, and The journey to the west*

標題： 1. Ts'ao, Hsueh-ch'in, ca. 1717–1763. Hung lou meng.

2. Wu, Ch'eng-en, ca. 1500–ca. 1582. Hsi yu chi.

3. Shui hu chuan.

4. Chinese literature—History and criticism.

5. Stone in literature.

6. Stone—Folklore.

書名: *The clouds should know me by now: Buddhist poet monks of China*

標題: Chinese poetry—Buddhist authors—Translations into English.

書名: *Gone with the wind*

標題: 1. Women—Georgia—History—19th century—Fiction.

2. Georgia—History—Civil War, 1861–1865—Fiction.

書名: *Margaret Mitchell: the book, the film, the woman*

標題: 1. Mitchell, Margaret, 1900–1949.

2. Mitchell, Margaret, 1900–1949. Gone with the wind.

3. Gone with the wind (Motion picture)

4. Women novelists, American—20th century—Biography.

5. Historical fiction, American—Authorship.

6. Georgia—History—Civil War, 1861–1865—Literature and the war.

7. Atlanta (Ga.)—Biography.

書名: *"Frankly my dear--": Gone with the wind memorabilia*

標題: 1. Mitchell, Margaret, 1900 –1949. Gone with the wind.

2. Gone with the wind (Motion picture)—Collectibles.

書名: *Margaret Mitchell*

標題: 1. Mitchell, Margaret, 1900–1949. Gone with the wind.

2. Historical fiction, American——History and criticism.

3. Women and literature——Georgia——History——20th century.

4. War stories, American——History and criticism.

5. Georgia——History——Civil War, 1861–1865——Literature and the war.

書名：*Coleridge, Lamb, Hazlitt, and the reader of drama*

標題： 1. Coleridge, Samuel Taylor, 1772–1834——Knowledge——Literature.

2. Lamb, Charles, 1775–1834——Knowledge——Literature.

3. Hazlitt, William, 1778–1830——Knowledge——Literature.

4. Dramatic criticism——Great Britain——History——19th century.

5. English drama——History and criticism.

書名：*Computers and the history of art*

標題： 1. Art——Historiography——Data processing.

2. Cataloging of art——Data processing.

書名：*An index to reproductions of paintings by twentieth -century Chinese artists*

標題： 1. Painting, Chinese——20th century——Indexes.

書名：*Leaves from a western garden: a magazine devoted to the Orient*

標題： 1. Civilization, Oriental——Periodicals.

2. Chinese literature——Periodicals.

書名：*The idea of the English landscape painter: genius as Alibi in the early nineteenth century*

標題： 1. Landscape painting, English.

2. Landscape painting--19th century--England.

書名： *A century in crisis: modernity and tradition in the art of twentieth-century China*

標題： 1. Art, Chinese--20th century--Themes, motives--Exhibitions.

書名： *Transience: Chinese experimental art at the end of the twentieth century*

標題： 1. Art, Chinese.

2. Art, Modern--20th century--China.

書名： *Along the riverbank: Chinese painting from the C. C. Wang family collection*

標題： 1. Wang, Chi-ch'ien--Art collections--Catalogs.

2. Painting, Chinese--Catalogs.

書名： *The Buddha scroll*

標題： 1. Ting, Kuan-p'eng, 18th cent. Fa chieh yuan liu t'u

2. Painting, Buddhist--China--Jilin Sheng

3. Painting, Chinese--Ming-Ch'ing dynasties, 1368–1912.

書名： *Art directory: galleries, alternative spaces, and resources in P. R. 〔Puerto Rico〕*

標題： 1. Art galleries, Commercial--Puerto Rico--Directories.

2. Alternative spaces (Arts facilities)--Puerto Rico--Directories.

3. Art--Puerto Rico--Information services--Directories.

書名： *Chinese opera: images and stories*

標題： 1. Operas, Chinese--History and criticism.

書名： *State sacrifices and music in Ming China: ortho-doxy, creativity, and expressiveness*

標題： 1. Rites and ceremonies--China.

2. Sacrifice--China.

3. Music--China--Religious aspects.

4. China--History--Ming dynasty, 1368--1644.

書名： *Harmony and counterpoint: ritual music in Chinese context*

標題： 1. Music--China--Religious aspects.

2. Rites and ceremonies--China.

書名： *From Confucius to Kublai Khan: music and poetics through the centuries*

標題： 1. Music--China--History and criticism.

2. Arts, Medieval--China.

書名： *A guide to Chinese music*

標題： Music--China--History and criticism.

社會科學 (SOCIAL SCIENCES):

書名： *Harvard China review*

標題： 1. China--Economic conditions--Periodicals.

2. China--Politics and government--Periodicals.

3. China--Social conditions--Periodicals.

書名： *The Blackwell dictionary of twentieth-century social thought*

標題： 1. Social sciences--History--20th century--Encyclopedias.

2. Philosophy--History--20th century--Encyclopedias.

3. Civilization, Modern--20th century--Encyclopedias.

書名： *The Wilson chronology of Asia and the Pacific*

標題： 1. Asia--History--Chronology.

2. Pacific Area--History--Chronology.

書名： *Did Marco Polo go to China?*

標題： 1. Polo, Marco, 1254–1323? Travels of Marco Polo.

2. Voyages and travels--Historiography.

3. China--Description and travel--History.

書名： *India, Pakistan, and the Kashmir tangle*

標題： 1. Jammu and Kashmir (India)--Politics and government.

2. India--Foreign relations--Pakistan.

3. Pakistan--Foreign relations--India.

書名： *The Yangtze*

標題： 1. Yangtze River (China)--Description and travel--Juvenile literature.

2. Yangtze River Valley (China)--Description and travel--Juvenile literature.

書名： *Taiwan*

標題： 1. Taiwan--Guidebooks.

2. Taiwan--History.

3. Taiwan--Description and travel.

書名： *The Realm of Jade Mountain: the ten top scenic spots of Taiwan, the Republic of China*

標題：　1. Landscape photography.

　　　　2. Taiwan––Description and travel.

書名：　*Hong Kong and Macao: the rough guide*

標題：　1. Hong Kong (China)––Guidebooks.

　　　　2. Macau (China: Special Administrative Region)––Guide-
　　　　books.

書名：　*The Boxer rebellion*

標題：　China––History––Boxer Rebellion, 1899–1901.

書名：　*What life was like in the land of the dragon: imperi-
al China, A.D. 960-1368*

標題：　1. China––Social life and customs––960–1644.

　　　　2. China––History––Sung dynasty, 960–1279.

　　　　3. China––History––Yuan dynasty, 1260–1368.

書名：　*The rise of modern Taiwan*

標題：　1. Taiwan––Politics and government––1945–

　　　　2. Taiwan––Economic conditions––1945–

　　　　3. Taiwan––Social conditions––1945–

　　　　4. Taiwan––Foreign relations––1945–

書名：　*The Wilson chronology of women's achievements: a
record of women's achievements from ancient times
to present*

標題：　Women––History––Chronology.

書名：　*The Hong Kong school curriculum: development, is-
sues, and policies*

標題：　1. Curriculum planning––China––Hong Kong.

2. Education––China––Hong Kong––Curricula.

3. Educational evaluation––China––Hong Kong.

書名： *The myth of the first three years: a new understanding of early brain development and lifelong learning*

標題： 1. Learning, Psychology of.

2. Educational psychology.

3. Pediatric neuropsychology.

書名： *Libraries and information centres in Hong Kong*

標題： 1. Libraries––China––Hong Kong––Directories.

2. Information services––China––Hong Kong––Directories.

書名： *Libraries and librarianship in China*

標題： Libraries––China.

書名： *Cataloging and classification: an introduction*

標題： 1. Cataloging––United States.

2. Classification––Books.

科學與技術 (SCIENCE AND TECHNOLOGY):

書名： *A dictionary of computing*

標題： 1. Electronic data processing––Dictionaries.

2. Computers––Dictionaries.

書名： *Computers and their applications: proceedings of the ISCA 13th international conference, Honolulu, Hawaii, U.S.A., March 25-27, 1998*

標題： 1. Application software––Congresses.

2. Computers––Congresses.

書名：*Introduction to mathematical finance: discrete time models*

標題：1. Finance--Mathematical models.

書名：*An introduction to mathematical logic*

標題：1. Logic, Symbolic and mathematical.

書名：*An introduction to mathematical fire modeling*

標題：1. Combustion--Mathematical models.

書名：*Proceedings of the Second International Workshop on ERS Applications: London, 6-8 December 1995*

標題：1. ERS-1 (Artificial satellite)--Congresses.

　　　2. Artificial satellites in earth sciences--Congresses.

　　　3. Artificial satellites in remote sensing--Congresses.

　　　4. Earth sciences--Remote sensing--Congresses.

書名：*Biophysics of photoreception: molecular and photo-transductive events: proceedings of the International School of Biophysics, Casamicciola, Napoli, Italy, 10-16 October 1994*

標題：1. Photoreceptors--Congresses.

　　　2. Biophysics--Congresses.

書名：*Statistical mechanics in physics and biology: symposium held December 2-5, 1996, Boston, Massachusetts, U.S.A.*

標題：1. Statistical mechanics--Congresses.

　　　2. Biophysics--Congresses.

書名：*Green nature/human nature: the meaning of plants*

in our lives

標題： Human-plant relationships.

書名： *Chemistry of arsenic, antimony, and bismuth*

標題： 1. Arsenic.

2. Antimony.

3. Bismuth.

書名： *CERN annual report/European Laboratory for Particle Physics*

標題： 1. European Laboratory for Particle Physics ——Periodicals.

2. Nuclear physics——Research——Periodicals.

書名： *Nuclear data sheets 〔computer file〕*

標題： 1. Nuclear physics——Tables——Periodicals.

書名： *Mozambique national mine survey*

標題： 1. Mines and mineral resources——Mozambique——Directories.

書名： *Whaley & Wong's nursing care of infants and children*

標題： 1. Pediatric nursing.

書名： *Overview of school health services: school nurse review*

標題： 1. School nursing——Handbooks, manuals, etc.

普通題目 (GENERAL/MISCELLANEOUS):

書名： *Little-known museums in and around Paris*

標題： 1. Museums——France——Paris——Guidebooks.

2. Paris (France)——Guidebooks.

書名：*Signs, symbols and icons: pre-history to the computer age*

標題：　1. Signs and symbols--History.

2. Nonverbal communication.

3. Computer graphics.

4. Computers and the handicapped.

書名：*Learning in an electronic world: computers and the language arts classroom*

標題：　1. Language arts (Elementary)--Computer-assisted instruction.

2. English language--Computer-assisted instruction.

3. Computer-assisted instruction.

書名：*In the eye of the beholder: the science of face perception*

標題：　1. Face perception.

書名：*Understanding movies*

標題：　1. Motion pictures.

書名：*Chocolate for breakfast and tea: B&B innkeepers share their finest recipes*

標題：　1. Cookery (Chocolate)

2. Baked products.

3. Breakfasts.

4. Bed and breakfast accommodations--United States--Directories.

書名：*The Market for physical fitness and exercise equip-*

ment

標題： 1. Exercise equipment industry--United States.

2. Market surveys--United States.

第八章　主題標目的參照

　　從主題標目的結構一章中，我們了解標題有各種不同的結構，在詞義相同或類似的詞語中，我們只能選擇其中的一個做標題，標題字的順序也影響到檢索者的檢索點(access point)。再從整個標題系統觀之，有涵義狹窄而專門的標題，有涵義廣泛而普通的標題，它們之間有縱的層次關係，也有橫的相關關係。這些錯綜複雜的關係，交織成阡陌狀的無形圖譜，如果沒有適當的指標來指點迷津，檢索者將無所適從，而標題的作用也將大為削弱。參照(cross reference)就是標題之間的指標，它的作用是指引檢索者從不同的檢索點逐步追尋到他們要找的標題。

　　國會圖書館的參照，於1986年在術語及結構上皆有重大的改變，1986出版的第十版《國會圖書館主題標目表》上的參照系統是舊有的辦法。我們在這章裡討論的「參照」是根據《主題編目手冊：主題標目》的最新辦法，也是從第十一版以來所採用的辦法。

　　國會圖書館的標題系統有下列幾種參照：

　　「使用」參照(use reference)

　　「參見」參照(see also reference)

　　一般參照(general see also reference)

　　標題引見專有名稱參照(subject-to-name reference)

　　我們將在這一章逐一探討它們的結構和功能。

一、「使用」參照 **❶**

1. 「使用」參照指引檢索者自未經採用的詞語找到採用的標題，它的代號是 USE。如：

> Bobber fishing
>> USE Bait fishing
>
> Fishing with natural bait
>> USE Bait fishing
>
> Float fishing, British
>> USE Bait fishing
>
> Ledgering (Fishing)
>> USE Bait fishing
>
> Livebait fishing
>> USE Bait fishing
>
> Still fishing
>> USE Bait fishing

同時在採用的標題之下列出所有未被採用的詞語，其代號是 UF，used for 的簡稱。如：

> Bait fishing
>> UF Bobber fishing
>>
>> UF Fishing with natural bait
>>
>> UF Float fishing, British

---

❶ Library of Congress, *Subject Cataloging Manual: Subject Headings,* 5 th. ed. (Washington, D.C.: Library of Congress, 1996), H373, pp. 1–4.

UF Ledgering (Fishing)

UF Livebait fishing

UF Still fishing

上面的結構表示 Bait fishing 是國會圖書館所採用的標題，它取代了其他6種意念上大致相同的詞語。換句話說，這6種詞語沒有被國會圖書館採用。

USE references 即相當於過去的 See references，而 UF 即過去的 See from（其代號是 X）。

2.如果採用的標題是屬於倒置標題，一定要有直敘式的標題做為「使用」參照。如：

Breakwaters, Mobile

UF Mobile breakwaters

反過來說，如果直敘標題在首字之外還有其他重要字眼(significant word)的話，也應使用倒置的辦法把這些重要的字眼置於詞首做為「使用」參照以便檢索。如：

Truck driving

UF Driving, Truck

Light sources

UF Sources of light

Business intelligence

UF Business espionage

UF Corporate intelligence

UF Espionage, Business

UF Espionage, Industrial

UF Industrial espionage

UF Intelligence, Business

UF Intelligence, Corporate

從上面的例子可以看出，利用「倒置」或「直敘」的方法把重要的字眼置於詞首的辦法，也可以適用在「使用」參照之間。如Business espionage 本身是使用參照之一，它的存在也連帶產生了另一個「使用」參照，Espionage, Business。因為 Espionage 是一個重要的字眼，也是一個極可能為檢索者所尋找的字眼。

3.變體拼音詞語，以及文法結構上的差異，也應成為「使用」參照的一部分。如:

Door knobs

UF Doorknobs

Cluster housing

UF Clustered housing

Glamour photography

UF Glamor photography

Historic farms

UF Historical farms

Serial publications

UF Serials (Publications)

Buses--Vandalism

UF Bus vandalism

4.「使用」參照有時也用來表示某些狹窄的意念，其本身不足以成為一個標題，而為意念較廣的標題所取代。如:

Children of single parents

UF Children of single fathers

UF Children of single mothers

Bait fishing

UF Worm fishing

5.如果縮寫字(abbreviations)、頭字語(acronyms)、起首字母(initials)成為標題的話，它所代表的完整拼音詞語即應做為「使用」參照。如：

MARC System

UF Machine-readable Catalog System

如果以完整拼音的詞語做為標題，通常就不必以它的縮寫字、頭字語或起首字母為「使用」參照。除非它們也是為人所熟知者。如：

Ammonium nitrate fuel oil

UF AN-FO

UF ANFO

6.如果以大眾所熟知的外國詞語做標題，要以相當的英語做「使用」參照。如：

Tofu（豆腐）

UF Bean curd

UF Soybean curd

一般英語的標題並不以外國詞語做為「使用」參照（專有名詞除外）。

7.如果一個標題以國名、種族名，或語言名稱做詞首時，應由其所形容的對象做「使用」參照。如：

Mexican American art

UF Art, Mexican American

如果國名、種族名或語言名稱不在詞首的位置，則應有以它們為

詞首的「使用」參照。如:

Art, French

UF French art

二、「參見」參照❷

「參見」參照有兩種:一種是顯示標題間之層次(hierarchy)的參照。它的作用是將層次較高的標題,亦即詞義較廣的標題(broader term,簡稱 BT)和層次較低,亦即詞義較狹窄的標題(narrower term,簡稱 NT)相互繫聯。

另一種是顯示標題之間的相關關係。

1.**層次參照**(hierarchical reference) 它的結構如下:

〔詞義較窄的標題〕

BT〔詞義較廣(高一層次)的標題〕

例子:

Hot dog rolls

BT Bread

Bread

NT Hot dog rolls

BT Baked products

BT 是層次繫聯的代號,它位於詞義較廣的標題之前。

「層次」一語是指標題涵義的廣窄。廣窄的標準可以具體的關係闡述於下:

(1)類別(class)與類屬(class member)的關係:

---

❷ 同❶,H370, pp. 1-12。

Apes

    NT Gorilla

    BT Primates

Women executives

    NT Minority women executives

    BT Executives

Dental anthropology

    BT Physical anthropology

Buildings, Prefabricated

    NT Prefabricated houses

    BT Industrialized building

Cinematography

    NT Television film

    BT Photography

⑵整體(whole)與部分(part)的關係：

Toes

    NT Toenails

    BT Foot

Ethnologh

    NT Race relaxions

    BT Anthropology

⑶總稱(generic topic)與專稱例子(proper-named example)的關係：

West Lake (China)

    BT Lakes-China

原則上每一個標題至少應有一個高一層次的參照，以顯示這個標

題和其他標題的關係。部分標題的層次是多元性的，因此需要較多層次參照來表示它的多元性，但為了經濟起見通常不超過三個。如：

Women college administrators

BT College administrators

Women executives

Women in education

唯有在下列的情況下，標題可以不必依規定有一個高一層次的參照：

⑴這個標題恰巧是一個「類」的最高層次。譬如：Science

⑵地區名稱。譬如：Asia; United States

⑶家族名稱。譬如：Wang family

⑷某些倒置標題。譬如：Art, French

2.相關詞語參照(related term reference)　相關詞語參照的代號是 RT。RT 是 related term 的簡稱，它的結構是：

〔第一個相關標題〕

RT〔第二個相關標題〕

〔第二個相關標題〕

RT〔第一個相關標題〕

主題編目部目前的政策是側重層次參照的發展，而抑制相關詞語參照，以免整個參照制度膨脹太快，形成尾大不掉，因此對相關詞語參照的設立限制甚嚴。相關詞語參照的設立僅限於下列三種情況：

⑴繫聯部分意念相同的兩個標題。如：

Boats and boating

RT Ships

Ships

RT Boats and boating

(2)繫聯學科(discipline)和它的對象(object)。如：

Ornithology

　　RT Birds

Birds

　　RT Ornithology

(3)繫聯職業和從業人員。如：

Medicine

　　RT Physicians

Physicians

　　RT Medicine

三、一般參照 ❸

　　前面兩節所討論的「使用」及「參見」參照，也可以說是特定參照(specific reference)，因為它們是特別為了某些特定標題而設立的。與特定參照情況不同的是這裡要討論的一般參照，它是為了一群或一類標題而設計的參照，也是為了提示檢索者而做的一般宣言。下面列舉數種最常見的一般參照，讀者不難從中體會其功能。

　　SA是 See Also 的簡稱。它提示檢索者不要忘了檢索各別複分及專有名詞。因為名稱繁多，無法一一列舉。

　　例一：

Taxation

　　SA subdivision Taxation under topical headings

---

❸　同❶，H317，pp. 1-9；H374，pp. 1-2。

它提示檢索者注意以稅收(taxation)做複分的標題。

例二:

Church buildings

SA Names of individual churches

它提示檢索者查尋教堂建築物要從個別教堂建築名稱著手。

例三:

Kidneys

SA heading beginning with the word Renal

它提示檢索者,其他有關腎臟的標題要從以 Renal 為字首的標題著手,如Renal artery, Renal pharmacoloqy等。

例四:

Exhibitions

SA Names of individual exhibitions and subdivision Exhibitions under subjects

這個例子較為複雜,它兼具了前面的幾種一般參照。

四、標題引見專有名稱參照❹

這種參照指引檢索者從一般標題標準檔(Subject Authority File)中找到和這一類主題相關的專有名稱。這種參照目前僅限於下列幾種:

1. 種族(ethnic groups)

Ethnology——China

NT Chuang (Chinese people)

Indians of North America

---

❹ 同❶,H375。

　　　　NT Eskimos

2. 建築物(buildings, structures, etc.)

　　Museums——Italy

　　　　NT Palazzo Madama (Turin, Italy)

　　Palaces——England

　　　　NT Buckingham Palace (England)

3. 地理形象(geographic features)

　　Mountains——China

　　　　NT T'ai Mountains (China)

　　Rivers——China

　　　　NT Yellow River (China)

第九章　圖書自動化資訊系統

一、美國國會圖書館資訊系統

美國國會圖書館於1961年與美國圖書館資源委員會(Council on Library Resources)合作,致力於探討廣泛使用電腦於國會圖書館的作業 ❶。經過數年的研究、試驗,終於在1966年製成了一套由電腦操作的圖書編目系統,稱為國會圖書館機讀式目錄(Library of Congress Machine Readable Catalog)。

早期的機讀式目錄資料庫不外是儲藏國會圖書館製作的圖書編目,專門為編目人員操作使用,讀者並不能利用它們來檢索資料。

1969年以後,國會圖書館開始供應機讀式編目磁帶 (Machine Readable Cataloging tape,簡稱 MARC tape) 給其他圖書館。在此之前外界需要國會圖書館的目錄卡片時,需逐一依據美國國會圖書館控制號碼(Library of Congress Control Number)求購,來回頗費時日。自從有了機讀式編目磁帶,只需成為長期磁帶訂戶,就可定期收到整套的機讀式編目磁帶。個別圖書館視本身的需要直接從磁帶擷取資料,省時、方便而效率高。

---

❶ Library of Congress, Professional Association, *Automation at the Library of Congress: Inside Views* (Washington, D.C.: Library of Congress Professional Association, 1986), p. 1.

到了1970年代，國會圖書館資訊系統(Library of Congress Information System)除了處理館內業務之外，進一步對讀者提供服務。這個系統主要是由兩個大單元構成：第一個單元稱為多用途機讀式目錄系統（Multiple Use MARC System，簡稱 MUMS）。第二個單元稱為主題內容檢索之電腦連線資訊處理系統（Subject-Content-Oriented Retriever for Processing Information Online，簡稱為 SCORPIO)。第二、三兩節將分別介紹這兩種資訊系統。

二、主題內容檢索之電腦連線資訊處理系統

SCORPIO 的電腦語言(computer language)使用ALC和 PL1，它的硬體是 IBM 3033和3084。目前國會圖書館約有3,000部終端機(terminal)及電腦印刷機(printer) ❷ 供館內人員及讀者使用。

SCORPIO 是為了一般沒有電腦經驗的使用者而設計的，因此它的電腦檢索指令(computer command)力求簡單 ❸ 。

SCORPIO 有以下幾個主要的資料檔 ❹：

1.國會圖書館電腦目錄(Library of Congress Computerized Catalog，簡稱 LCCC)

這個資料檔貯藏國會圖書館的書籍(book)目錄。1968年以來英文書籍的編目都貯藏在這個資料檔中。其他語文的書籍陸續的在不同的時間貯藏於這個系統：

---

❷ Library of Congress, *Introducing LOCIS: SCORPIO* (Washington, D.C.: Library of Congress, 1987), p. 5.

❸ 同❷，p. 7。

❹ 同❷，pp. 2–5。

法文	1973年以後編目的書籍
德文、葡文、西班牙文	1975年以後編目的書籍
其他西歐語文	1976年以後編目的書籍
羅馬化的 Cyrillic 語	1979年以後編目的書籍
南亞語文	1979年以後編目的書籍
其他非羅馬字語文	1980年以後編目的書籍

每一本書籍的款目包括著作者、書名、出版者、出版地點、時間、主題標目、國會圖書館索書號、國會圖書館卡片編號以及其他資料。

使用者可以從著作者、書名、主題標目或索書號來檢索書籍。

2.早於國會圖書館機讀式目錄之前的目錄(PREMARC)

這項亦為機讀式的目錄，是 LCCC 的補充。它包涵前項電腦目錄沒有收錄的早期書籍，以及1968年以前編目的地圖，1984年以前編目的音樂記錄。它的款目和前項電腦目錄大致相同，惟較簡略。

3.聯合國(United Nations)出版物中選出的有關公共政策(public policy)和新近時事(current affairs)的文章

這個資料檔只貯存書目，如果要閱讀全文則需進一步使用館中另一種稱為「光碟」(optical disk)的貯存系統。

每一項款目包括著作者、文章的標題、刊載文章的刊物名稱、它的卷數、頁數和年代，以及文章摘要。

4.立法資訊檔(Legislative Information File)

這個資訊檔貯存著1973年以來美國國會的立法資訊。亦即是國會圖書館研究服務部(Library of Congress Research Services)所出版的刊物"Digest of Public General Bills and Resolutions"的自動化檔案。

這項資訊檔可從法案號碼(bill number)、法案標題、法案提議人

(sponsor)、贊助人(cosponsor)、主題等項目著手檢索。

它的標題稱為立法索引詞語(Legislative Indexing Vocabulary Terms)。

5.版權歷史檔(Copyright History Monographs File)

這裡貯藏著向國會圖書館申請著作權的書籍、音響記錄，以及其他文藝創作品的記錄。每一項目包括作者姓名、版權申請人(copyright claimant)、著作標題、創作及申請版權時間等。

檢索者可以從作者、申請人、創作標題，以及註冊號碼從事檢索。

6.全國查詢中心總檔(National Referral Center Master File)

這個資料檔貯存全國14,000個自願對公眾提供有關科技和社會學文獻的組織和機關的資料。

每一項款目包括組織機關的名稱、地址、電話，以及它們的專長、文獻收藏、出版刊物、服務項目等。

檢索者可從組織機關名稱，或主題兩項著手。它的索引稱為"NRCM Thesaurus"，是專門為這項資料檔所設計的索引表。

三、多用途機讀式目錄系統

多用途機讀式目錄系統的電腦語言和硬體與前述的主題內容檢索之電腦線上資料處理系統相同。

它主要是為了編目及其他館內作業而設計的，它的資料檔大部分是電腦線上作業，也就是說它的內容是隨時增刪修訂的。為了提高效率，它的檢索指令較前述的系統要複雜得多❺。

多用途機讀式目錄系統有7種不同的資料檔❻：

1.書籍檔(Book File)

書籍檔之下又可以再細分成5種不同用途的資料檔:

(1)書籍總檔(Books Master File)

這個資料檔的內容和 SCORPIO 裡的 LCCC 檔相同，因此不再重述。

(2)自動化處理資訊檔(Automated Process Information File)

這裡記錄著資料在編目時的每一個步驟，館內人員可以利用記錄追蹤每一項正在編目的資料，資料編目到了什麼程度? 目前停留在什麼單位? 何人經手等消息，皆可一目了然。

(3)圖書館訂購資訊系統(Library Order Information System)

這項檔案，提供國會圖書館訂購圖書的資訊。國會圖書館的圖書來源很多，訂購者僅代表整個來源較少的一部分，所以這項檔案並不能視為整個國會圖書館圖書來源的完整記錄。

(4)國家聯合目錄(National Union Catalog)

這裡記錄著從1982年以來其他圖書館編目而繳存於國會圖書館的圖書。這些書籍不限於任何語言或任何出版地點，其中部分是國會圖書館本身藏書中所沒有的。

(5)全國其他藏書所記錄(National Register of Additional Locations)

顧名思義這裡記載國內其他圖書館的庋藏。這項記載肇始於1968年，記錄1954年以後出版的圖書。

2.期刊檔(Serials File)

期刊檔成立於1973年，其目的是匯錄國會圖書館以及其他圖書館

---

❺　Library of Congress, *Introducing LOCIS: MUMS* (Washington, D.C.: Library of Congress, 1987), p. 6.

❻　同❺，pp. 2–5。

期刊的資料,俾使其發展成為全國性的總期刊目錄。

3.地圖檔(Maps File)

地圖檔存錄國會圖書館1968年以來的地圖資料,1985年以後它也擴大範圍收錄其他圖書館的地圖資料。它的檔案包括單張地圖(sheet map)、凸版地圖模型(relief model)、地球儀(globe),但不包括地圖集(atlas),地圖集歸於書籍總檔。

4.音樂檔(Music File)

此處收錄國會圖書館自1984年以來編目的樂譜、手稿,以及錄音資料。有關音樂的書籍和期刊分別記錄於書籍總檔和期刊檔。

5.視聽資料檔(Audiovisual Materials File)

視聽資料包括國會圖書館1972年以來編目的幻燈片(slide)、條狀底片(film strip)、透明圖片(transparency)、影片、錄影帶(videorecording)、照片(photograph)、圖片(drawing)等。

6.早於國會圖書館機讀式目錄之前的目錄(PREMARC)

此項目錄與前述 SCORPIO 裡的 PREMARC 內容相同,不再重複介紹。

7.近東國家聯合目錄(Near East National Union List)

這裡記錄1979年以前,美國和加拿大240個機關所收藏有關阿拉伯、波斯、土耳其語文的書籍與期刊。

8.標準檔(Authority Files)

標準檔包括名稱標準檔(Name Authority File),以及標題標準檔(Subject Authority File)。前者是著錄時有關個人、公司、機關、行政區域名稱的標準檔。後者是主題編目時所編製的標題標準檔,也是第八章中所提到的標題標準檔。這兩項標準檔完全是為了編目工作而建立的,也是著錄編目員和主題編目員每日不可或缺的工具。名稱標準

檔的例子請參閱表9-1。

表9-1

```
001   n81-114057
040   DLC DLC
100   Ping-hsin, 1900– 〔AACR 2〕
400   Hsieh, Wan-ying, 1902– 〔old catalog heading〕〔do not make〕
400   Bingxin, 1900–
400   Hsieh, Wan-ying, 1900–
400   Hsieh, Ping-hsin, 1900–
400   Nan-shih, 1900–
400   Hsieh, Shui-hsin, 1900–
400   Wu Hsien, Wan-ying, 1900–
400   Xie, Bingxin, 1900–
670   Her Spring water, 1922?
670   Chung-kuo hsien tai tso chia chuan 1uen, 1979 (Ping-hsin, b. 10/5/1900)
670   Bartels, W. Xie Bingxin, Leben und Werk in der Volksrepublik China, 1982: t. p. (Xie Bingx-
      in) p. 10 (Bing xin; orig. name, Xie Wanying; also known as Xie Xinglang when young)
960   AOC AMC NUC ACN
985   KEY/EKI
```

四、Integrated Library System

前面所介紹的自動化系統，都是30年前左右的產物，已經不能勝任國會圖書館日益繁重的多元化任務。有鑑於此，國會圖書館在1997年8月成立了一個稱為"Integrated Library System Program Office"，來主持自動化系統的大改進，冀使國會圖書館在21世紀來臨之時，能夠有一套新式的自動系統，迎接新時代的挑戰。

Integrated Library System，簡稱 ILS，就是「圖書館自動化一貫作業系統」。它的作用是圖書館從採購、出納、編目，到提供目錄給讀者使用、借書、還書，一切圖書館日常的作業，完全融貫在一個電

腦資訊系統上。

目前的 ILS 工作室有20個工作人員全力投入工作。另有560個員工分屬18個工作委員會對此項工程提供技術援助。

在1999年1月，這個命名為 Voyager 的 ILS 自動化系統，已成功地輸入了12萬項圖書目錄，4萬項名稱以及主題標準檔。已有450個終端機連接在這個系統上（使用Window 95, Pentium 300 MHz）。這項工程期待在1999年10月完工。屆時將有2,000部終端機連接在這項系統上。在本書撰稿時（1999年5月），編目部的員工正在進行編目實驗。如果進行順利，借書部門、查詢部門以及期刊部門，也將逐步投入這項一貫作業的自動化系統 ❼ 。

有關這項系統的訊息，請查閱：http://www.loc.gov/ils。

五、Cataloger's Desk Top and Classification Plus

國會圖書館在近年對編目工具書自動化上有重大的突破。1997年問世的 Cataloger's Desk Top，以及相繼問世的 Classification Plus 將所有重要的編目工具書完全歸納在兩項 CD-ROM系統下。使用者可以有效地利用電腦操作來查閱各種編目規章，既便捷又省錢，是新時代圖書館必具的兩項資訊系統。

Cataloger's Desk Top 包括以下的工具書：

• *Anglo-American Cataloguing Rules* (2nd. ed., 1998 Revision)

• *Library of Congress Rule Interpretations*

---

❼ Library of Congress, *Integrated Library System Program* (Washington D.C., Library of Congress Homepage, 1999), pp. 1–2.

- *Subject Cataloging Manual: Subject Headings*, 5th. ed. (1996) with direct access to LCSH Free-floating Subdivisions, and LCSH Pattern Headings
- *Subject Cataloging Manuals: Classification & Shelflisting*
- *USMARC Format for Bibliographic Data*
- *USMARC Format for Authority Data*
- *USMARC Format for Holdings Data*
- *USMARC Format for Classification Data*
- *USMARC Format for Community Information*
- *Latest editions of all 5 USMARC Code Lists*
- *Archival Moving Image Materials*
- *Cataloging Rules for the Description of Looseleaf Pubs.*
- *CONSER Cataloging Manual*
- *CONSER Editing Guide*
- *Graphic Materials: Rules for Describing Original Items and Historical Collections*
- *Map Cataloging Manual*
- *Music Cataloging Decisions*
- *Standard Citation Forms for Published Bibliographies Used in Rare Book Cataloging*
- *Thesaurus for Graphic Materials*
- *Descriptive Cataloging Manual-Z1: Names and Series Authority Records*
- *LC Cutter Table* (as a separate infobase)
- *Library of Congress Filing Rules*
- *NACO Participants' Manual*, 2nd ed. (1996)

Classification Plus 包括以下的工具書：

- *Library of Congress Classification Schedules*
- *Library of Congress Subject Headings*

有關國會圖書館編目工具書的資料可以查詢以下的網路：http://www.loc.gov/cds。

六、RLG/CJK 系統

前面數節論及的自動化資訊作業，都是以羅馬語文資料(roman language materials)為主。在過去，中、日、韓等文字的圖書編目都經過羅馬字化(romanized)以後才能輸入國會圖書館電腦系統，其短處顯而易見的是使用者很難明瞭羅馬字所替代的原文。

表9-2是二項中文編目，經過羅馬字化之後在 MARC 的記錄：

表9-2

〔MUMS〕   4

PL2722. U2L53495 1982 Orien China

AACR2

Liu, Hsin-chung.

* Tuan p'ien hsiao shuo chih wang: "Liao chai chih i" man t'an/Liu Hsin-chung. ––Ti 1 pan. Shih-chia-chuang shih: Hua shan wen i ch'u pan she: Ho-pei sheng hsin hua shu tien fa hsing, 1982.

196 p.; 19 cm.

RMBY0. 52 (pbk.)

10/25/87   unb   chi   83–137880

〔MUMS〕

PL2727. S2P4 1984 Orien China

AACR2

Pi, Shu-min.

* Hung lou meng k'ao lun chi/Pi Shu-min chu. ––Ch'u pan. ––T'ai-pei shih: Lien ching ch'u pan shih yeh kung ssu, min kuo 73

〔1984〕

4, 2, 186 p.; 22 cm.

CJK
RS
NT$100.00

10/25/87　　　　　chi　　85-125059

中文應用於電腦上有許多技術上的困難，到了70年代隨著電腦技術的日新月異，中文自動化處理系統乃突破困限，成為事實。

國會圖書館為了解除識別羅馬化字音的困難，俾便使用者能夠直接在終端機螢幕上看到中、日、韓原文，乃於1979年和座落於加州史丹佛大學(Stanford University)校區內的研究圖書館組織(Research Libraries Group，簡稱RLG)簽訂合約，由 RLG 研究發展可以同時處理中、日、韓文以及羅馬字的自動化圖書館處理系統。經過4年的研究，RLG 於1983年達成了任務。同年的春天，國會圖書館開始試用這項稱為 RLG/CJK 的自動化處理系統，CJK 是 Chinese、Japanese 及 Korean 的簡稱 [8]。

RLG/CJK 的硬體和其他自動化資訊系統大同小異，其特色是在鍵盤(keyboard)上。它有179個字鍵，其中133個是文字鍵(character key)，36個是作用鍵(function key)，10個是控制鍵(control key)。文字鍵包括245個漢字的偏旁，96個日文 katakana 與 hiragana 偏旁，以及33個韓文 Hangul 字母 [9]。漢字和韓文 Hangul 字的組成是在終端機螢幕底線的造字欄上運用偏旁的組合而構成完整的字。除了上述特別的字鍵，它也具有一般文字自動處理系統上所有的羅馬字與阿拉伯數

---

[8]　Library of Congress, *Library of Congress Information Bulletin* (Washington, D.C.: Library of Congress, March 26, 1982), p. 95.

[9]　Library of Congress, *Library of Congress Information Bulletin* (Washington, D.C.: Library of Congress, June 27, 1983), p. 216.

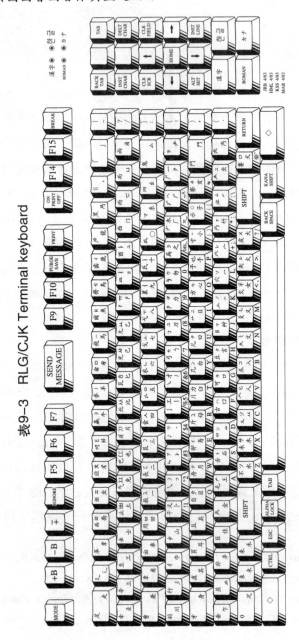

表9-3　RLG/CJK Terminal keyboard

字。為了利用有限的字鍵處理多種用途，一個字鍵常常兼具數種任務，隨著作用鍵的轉換而改變它的任務。鍵盤的結構請見表9-3。

每4具終端機繫聯成一組，由一控制機(controller)負責控制運作。控制機以電話線和遠在加州的 RLG 總部連線。每一組各有一具印刷機，可以隨時印出儲藏在系統裡的資料。

在漢字處理上 RLG/CJK 的特色有三：第一，單字是由偏旁依一定的次序組合而成。偏旁的選擇以及結構的次序往往有不合中國文字結構的邏輯，並有許多牽強與乖謬之組合，這是它最大的缺失。第二，漢字的輸入是以詞(word)或詞組(term)為輸入單位，而不以漢語單字(character)為輸入單位。譬如說「大學」、「朝代」、「改造」等詞在輸入時要把大學這兩個單字構成的詞連成一組輸入，同樣的朝代兩個單字要連成一組，改造兩個單字也要連成一組。而「圖書館」、「大學生」等詞組也是三字連成詞組輸入。檢索時，使用者必需依詞或詞組的方式來檢索。如果檢索者不熟知詞或詞組的繫聯法，檢索時會發生困難。因為電腦的索引(index)是根據輸入的詞或詞組來記憶和貯存，而不是根據單字來貯存。如果把「大學生」分成三個字來檢索，電腦無法找到「大學生」這一個詞組。同樣的，漢語詞或詞組的羅馬化拼音也必需繫聯成組。其方法是以「◇」的記號把羅馬字繫聯成組，如：ta◇hsüeh, ch'ao◇tai, t'u◇shu◇kuan，及 ta◇hsüeh◇sheng。至於詞或詞組的結構方法，是根據RLG出版的《漢字繫聯指引》(*RLG Chinese Aggregation Guidelines*)[10]。由於中國人習慣以單字為書寫的基本單位，書本印刷也沒有將單字繫聯成詞或詞組的習慣，加以繫聯的方法，見仁見智，並沒有行諸四海皆準的規則。上

---

[10] The Research Libraries Group, *RLG Chinese Aggregation Guidelines* (Stanford, Calif.: RLG, 1987).

述的指導原則亦僅侷限於 RLG/CJK 這個系統。使用者必需先熟習這些繫聯的原則，才能運用自如。

　第三個特點是它具有輸入「繁體字」與簡體字的能力。大部分繁體字可經由「作用鍵」而改換成簡體字。這個系統的繁簡字是同時並存的。如果所編目的書籍使用繁體字，則以繁體字編目，所編目的書籍使用簡體字，則編目亦用簡體字。這種依書籍本身的字體做編目字體的依據，而不拘泥於任何一種形式，未嘗不是解決棘手問題的最佳辦法。

　前面列舉的兩項羅馬化目錄在 RLG/CJK 系統的面貌如下：

劉　欣中，

　短篇　小說　之王：《聊齋　志異》漫談 / 劉　欣中，--第一版，--石家庄市：

　花山　文藝　出版社：河北省　新華　書店　發行，1982.

　196 p. ; 19 cm.

　Includes bibliographical references.

　RMBY0. 52 (pbk.)

　1.蒲　松齡，1640–1715. 聊齋　志異，I. Title.

　LCCN: 83137880/ACN/r88

　L. C. CALL NO: PL2722., U2L53495 1982 <Orien China>

　ID: DCLP84–B4047

　CC: 9114 DCF: a〔CJK〕

劉　述民，

　紅樓夢　考論　集 / 皮　述民　著，--初版，--臺北市：聯經　出版事業　公司，民國　73〔1984〕

4, 2, 186 p.; 22 cm.

Includes bibliographical references.

NT$100.00

1.曹　雪芹，ca. 1717–1763.　紅樓夢，I. Title.

LCCN: 85125059/ACN/r88

L. C. CALL NO: PL2727. S2. P4 1984 <Orien China>

ID: DCLP85–B5027　　　　　　　　　CC: 9114　DCF: a　〔CJK〕

以上介紹的 RLG/CJK 系統維持了十餘年，直到1997年這項系統開始採用新型 Window 電腦，鍵盤也改用一般的英文打字鍵盤。除了以漢字的形體來造字，也可以利用 Wade-Giles 及拼音來造字。更進一步利用四聲來分辨，造字更為便捷。目前使用的系統是1999年2月問世的軟體，稱為"RLIN Terminal for Windows, Version 5"。它是多用途的電腦，除了編目，也可以同時查詢名稱及主題標準檔，也具備剪裁、複製、館際互借(Interlibrary loan)的功能。

目前 RLG 系統儲藏3,200萬本書籍，包括365種語言。中文書籍有1,089,260件，韓文160,400件，日文807,280件。

加入 RLG/CJK 系統的大學及研究單位有：

University of Alberta

Arizona State University

University of British Columbia

University of California, Santa Barbara

Hoover Institution, Stanford University

University of California, Berkeley

Freer/Sackler Library

Library of Congress

University of Hawaii

University of Iowa

University of Chicago

Harvard-Yenching Library, Harvard University

University of Michigan

University of Minnesota

Nelson-Atkins

Duke University

Gest Oriental Library, Princeton University

Rutgers University

Cornell University

C. V. Starr East Asian Library, Columbia University

University of Toronto

University of Pennsylvania

School of Oriental and African Studies

Brigham Young University

Gallagher Law Library, University of Washington

有關 RLG 的資料，請查閱：http://www.rlg.org。

七、OCLC/CJK 系統

OCLC 是 Online Computer Library Center, Inc. 的簡稱。它座落在 Dublin, Ohio, USA，是一個非營利性質的機構，專門為圖書館和研究單位提供電腦網路服務。

目前有63個國家的23,000所圖書館和它直接連線。它提供編目、

查詢資料、採買、館際互借，以及為顧客將卡片式目錄改編成電腦機讀式目錄等服務。它是美國最大的圖書館電腦連線服務機構。

OCLC/CJK 系統是 OCLC 網下的一個分支，專門處理中、日、韓文字。前述 RLIN/CJK 是美國第一個處理中日韓文電腦連線的圖書服務機構。OCLC/CJK 系統比 RLIN-CJK 系統晚了幾年，到1987年才問世，但以其雄厚的 OCLC 資源基礎，目前與 RLIN/CJK 在處理中日韓文上成二雄對峙的形勢。OCLC/CJK 在它的聯合目錄上藏有170萬件中、日、韓文目錄。

OCLC/CJK 目前最新的軟體是稱為"OCLC CJK 3.0"的系統，使用"Microsoft Windows NT"。

它於1998年年底在美國8所大學進行實驗，1999年4月正式問世。對中文而言，它的特點是可以使用 Wade-Giles 或拼音來創造漢字。它的目錄是以 Wade-Giles 為基礎，但可以「按鈕」把它轉成拼音式的目錄。

加入 OCLC/CJK 系統的大學及研究單位有：

AsiaLink (OCLC)

Australian National University

Bruggemeyer Memorial Library

Chicago Public Library

Chinese University of Hong Kong

Duke University Library

Emory University General Libraries

Georgetown University

Harvard-Yenching Library, Harvard University

Hong Kong Polytechnic Library

Hong Kong University of Science & Technology

Indiana University

Institute for Advanced Studies of World Religion

Japan Foundation & Language Center

King County Library System

Library of Congress

Los Angeles Public Library

Nanyang Technological University

National Taiwan Normal University

National University of Singapore Library

Oberlin College

Ohio State University Libraries

Ohio University-Alden Library

Queens Borough Public Library

San Francisco Public Library

San Jose Public Library

Smith College Libraries

Soka University of America

St. John's University Library

University of Arizona

University of California at Berkeley

University of California at Davis

University of California at Irvine

University of California at Los Angeles

University of California at Riverside

University of California at San Diego

University of Colorado at Boulder

University of Illinois at Urbana-Champaign

University of Kansas

University of Maryland at College Park

University of Massachusetts at Amherst

University of North Carolina at Chapel Hill

University of Oregon

University of Pittsburgh

University of San Francisco

University of Southern California

University of Texas at Austin

University of Virginia

University of Washington

University of Wisconsin at Madison

Washington University

World Mission University

　　有關 OCLC 的資料，請查閱：http://www.oclc.org。

　　在此順便需要提出來的是美國圖書館界過去數十年來一向使用 Wade-Giles 音譯系統把中文字羅馬化，國會圖書館在1997年宣佈將在公元2000年時使用中國的拼音系統來取代 Wade-Giles 系統，其他美國東亞圖書館也將一一效法。目前國會圖書館正忙於將名稱、主題標準檔，以及有關中國部分的分類表改換成拼音系統，以迎接公元2000年將正式使用的拼音系統。

第十章　主題編目作業的主要工具

　　在主題編目作業的過程中，隨時需要使用工具書籍。舉凡分析資料內容、擬定標題、說明標題來源、確定參照層次、研製分類號碼，都離不開查考稽核的工夫。工具書籍大致可以分為兩種，一種是不可或缺的編目工具，另一種是備而待用的參考工具。本章的用意就是介紹這兩種主題編目所需的工具。

一、不可或缺的編目工具

　　這些編目工具可想而知地都是編目處所編製的產品，它們是使用國會圖書館主題編目制度者遵循的準則。

　　1.《國會圖書館主題標目表》(*Library of Congress Subject Headings*)

　　每年修訂出版一次。這是主題編目者研擬標題時必備的工具。

　　《國會圖書館主題標目表》的主要內容如下：

　　⑴主題標目(subject heading)

　　依字母的次序以醒目的粗體字(boldface type)排列。標題的第一個字母大寫，其餘的字小寫。例如：

　　　　Education

Information storage and retrieval systems

如果是倒置標題，則倒置詞語的第一個字母大寫，如：

Education, Compulsory

Coins, Ancient

括弧裡的第一個字大寫，如：

Cruisers (Warships)

Similarity (Geometry)

Framing (Building)

專有名詞一律大寫，如：

Pennsylvania Dutch Country (Pa.)

Yangtze River (China)

Yao Language (Southeastern Asia)

頭字語(acronym)一律用大寫，如：

MARC formats

IBM AS 400 (Computer)

⑵地區複分(geographic subdivision)

如果標題之後可以使用地區複分（參閱第六章第二節），則地區複分的代號 May Subd Geog 會以括弧的方式緊跟在標題之後，例如：

County government (May Subd Geog)

Mass media (May Subd Geog)

⑶類號(class number)

大約有百分之三十左右的標題之後附有國會圖書館分類號，以便分類。如果一個標題可以有幾個不同的類號，這些類號也逐一列出，如：

Shellfish

〔QL 401–QL 445 (Zoology)〕

〔RA 602. S2 (Public health)〕

〔TX 387 (Shellfish as food)〕

〔TX 753 (Cookery)〕

⑷使用範圍註釋(scope note)

　某些標題之下附有使用範圍註釋。它是為了提示使用者有關標題的涵義，該標題和其他類似標題之間的異同。試舉一例如下：

Social service

　Here are entered works on the methods employed in welfare work, public or private. Work on taxsupported welfare activities are entered under public welfare. Works on privately supported welfare activities are entered under charities.

⑸參照(cross reference)

　標題的參照（參閱第八章）均依 UF, BT, RT, SA, NT 的次序一一排列於標題之下，以便參考查閱。參照使用細體字編排。

⑹複分(subdivision)

　複分緊接在參照之下，依複分的字母次序排列（參閱第六章）。複分的第一個字母大寫，前面所述的標題大寫原則亦適用於複分。通用複分通常不再列於標題之下，如果複分之後可以使用地區複分，則地區複分的代號 May Subd Geog 以括弧的形式緊接於該項複分之後。如：

Management (May Subd Geog)

--Research (May Subd Geog)

Mines and mineral resources (May Subd Geog)

--Taxation (May Subd Geog)

主題標目表實際的編排式樣見表10-1。

表10-1

Buddhist hymns, English（*May Subd Geog*）
UF English Buddhist hymns
Buddhist hymns, Japanese（*May Subd Geog*）
UF Japanese Buddhist hymns
Buddhist hymns, Korean（*May Subd Geog*）
UF Korean Buddhist hymns
Buddhist hymns, Sinhalese（*May Subd Geog*）
UF Sinhalese Buddhist hymns
Buddhist idealism
USE Yogācāra (Buddhism)
Buddhist illumination of books and manuscripts
USE Illumination of books and manuscripts, Buddhist
Buddhist incantations
UF Incantations, Buddhist
NT Bonpo incantations
Buddhist dhāraṇī
Buddhist mantras
Buddhist inscriptions
USE Inscriptions, Buddhist
Buddhist interpretations of the Bible
USE Bible—Buddhist interpretations
Buddhist iron sculpture
USE Iron sculpture, Buddhist
Buddhist laity
USE Buddhist laymen
Buddhist laymen（*May Subd Geog*）
UF Buddhist laity
Lay Buddhists
Upāsaka
Upāsikā
BT Laity
—Discipline
[*BQ5485-BQ5530*]
NT Five Precepts (Buddhism)

Buddhist legends
  USE Legends, Buddhist
Buddhist literature (*May Subd Geog*)
  BT Religious literature
  NT Bonpo literature
    Buddhism—Sacred books
    Buddhist drama
    Buddhist poetry
    Buddhist sermons
    Sanskrit literature, Buddhist Hybrid
    Zen literature
—**Relation to the New Testament**
  UF Bible. N.T. —Relation to Buddhist literature
  BT Bible. N.T. —Criticism, interpretation, etc.
    Christianity and other religions—Buddhism
Buddhist literature, Bengali (*May Subd Geog*)
  UF Bengali Buddhist literature
  BT Bengali literature
Buddhist literature, Burmese (*May Subd Geog*)
  UF Burmese Buddhist literature
  BT Burmese literature
Buddhist literature, Chinese (*May Subd Geog*)
  UF Chinese Buddhist literature
  BT Chinese literature
Buddhist literature, Japanese (*May Subd Geog*)
  UF Japanese Buddhist literature
  BT Japanese literature
Buddhist literature, Korean (*May Subd Geog*)
  UF Korean Buddhist literature
  BT Korean literature
Buddhist literature, Manchu (*May Subd Geog*)
  UF Manchu Buddhist literature
  BT Manchu literature

　　這部工具書因為體積龐大，印製耗時而所費不貲，在1988年以前每隔幾年才能印製新的版本。在新版本出版之前，編目策劃及技援室另行刊印補充本，稱為《國會圖書館主題標目補充本》(*Supplement to L. C. Subject Headings*)。補充本每季出版一期，每年又將4本季刊合併成年刊。它們是原版本的延續，其重要性不亞於主題標目表本身。編目時必須連同補充本一道使用，才能確定所選擇的標題是正確而合宜的。1988年以後，第十一版以電腦儲存的標題標準檔為依據而編製標目表。編目處藉標準檔電腦作業之便，每年出版新的標目表，使得標目表能夠每年維持最新面貌。目前最新的標目表有5大冊。

2.主題標準檔(Subject Authority File)

這是由電腦儲存的主題標準檔。前面提到的主題標目表即是電腦主題標準檔的印刷版，唯其不同之處是編排的方式，主題標目表是按標題的字母次序排列，而標題標準檔是根據標題成立的先後排列的，並不依照標題的字母次序排列。每一項標準檔配備一個號碼叫主題標準號碼(Subject Authority Number)。在運用上兩者也因編排的不同而有所不同。主題標目表適合日常編目檢尋適當的標題而用，主題標準檔因為並非依照標題的字順排列，所以不能用來做為日常編目檢尋標題之用，它的特點是它包括所有最新近成立的標題。如果編目者對某一特定標題有疑問，需要稽核的話，標題標準檔是最可靠的查詢工具。例子見表10-2。

表10-2

-- 010 001 ≠ a ≠ sh85-75772

-- 020 040 ≠ ac ≠ DLC ≠ DLC

-- 030 150-0 ≠ a ≠ Legalism (Chinese philosophy)

-- 040 053 ≠ a ≠ B127. L43

-- 050 450-0 ≠ wa ≠ nnnn ≠ Legalist school of Chinese philosophy

-- 060 550-0 ≠ wa ≠ gnnn ≠ Philosophy, Chinese

-- 070 005 ≠ a ≠ 19860410130254.5

-- 080 FFD 01.n 02.i 　　03.0　　　04.a　　　　05.a　　　　06.n　07.n

　　　　　08.n 09.a 　　10.a　　　11.a　　　　12.b　　　　13.a　14.–

　　　　　15.b 16.a 　　17.b　　　18.n　　　　19.n　　　　20.a　21.a

　　　　　22.a 23.8150 24.fk05　25.-----　　26.-----　　27.–　28.–

　　　　　29.– 30.– 　　31.–　　　32.–　　　　33.7　　　　34.ǃ　35.7

　　　　　36.ǃ 37.ꞮꞮꞮ 　38.j　　　39.j　　　　40.4　　　　41.z　42.81

　　　　　43.a 44.n

3.《編目服務公報》(*Cataloging Service Bulletin*)

　　這是資料作業部出版的季刊，它對資料作業部所管轄的單位在過去4個月來有關規章的增刪修訂以及各單位的活動提供詳盡的報導。有了它，編目者才能掌握編目有關事項的最新動態，對編目工作者助益甚大。見表10-3。

表10-3

ISSN 0160-8029

LIBRARY OF CONGRESS/WASHINGTON

CATALOGING SERVICE BULLETIN

LIBRARY SERVICES
Number 83, Winter 1999
Editor: Robert M. Hiatt

CONTENTS

	Page
GENERAL	
LC to Implement Core-Level Cataloging	2
Program for Cooperative Cataloging Identification Code	12
DESCRIPTIVE CATALOGING	
Library of Congress Rule Interpretations	14
Headings for Conventional Chinese Place Names	40

Editorial postal address: Cataloging Policy and Support Office, Library Services, Library of Congress, Washington, D.C. 20540−4305

Editorial electronic mail address: CPSO@loc.gov

Editorial fax number: (202) 707−6629

Subscription address: Customer Support Team, Cataloging Distribution Service, Library of Congress, Washington, D.C. 20541−4912

Subscription electronic mail address: cdsinfo@loc.gov

Library of Congress Catalog Card Number: 78−51400

ISSN 0160−8029 ***Key title****:* Cataloging service bulletin

4.《主題編目手冊: 主題標目》(*Subject Cataloging Manual: Subject Headings*)

這部於1984年初版的主題編目規章，可以說是主題編目的「經典」，相當於著錄編目的《英美編目規則》(*Anglo-American Cataloguing Rules*)。對於學習國會圖書館主題編目規章者或實際使用國會圖書館編目制度者而言，這是領會國會圖書館主題編目的捷徑。目前最新的版本是1998年的第五版。它經常有不定期的修訂。

它對書籍在不同的內容或形式之下應該使用什麼標題做詳盡的闡釋。每一節通常都舉例說明，大部分是編目的實例，小部分是假設的

例子。在比較複雜的情況下，它還提供背景或歷史說明，使編目者能夠了解過去和現在對處理某項資料之遞嬗演變。因為這一章的重要性，我們特別把它的綱要存錄在附錄九上，以便使用者能夠略窺這一手冊的面貌。由於個別編目規章過於龐雜，本書略而不載。

5.《**國會圖書館分類表**》(*Library of Congress Classification Schedules*)

全表多達45冊，總頁數超過10,000頁，它是研擬國會圖書館分類制度必備的工具。它的細節擬於日後以專書討論，故不在此詳述。它的形式請見表10-4。

表10-4

SOCIAL SCIENCES (GENERAL)

	Social sciences (General)
	Periodicals. Serials
1.A1–A2	Polyglot
1.A3–Z	American and English
3	French
5	German
7	Italian
8.A–Z	Other languages, A–Z
9	Yearbooks
	Societies
10	International
11	American and English
13	French
15	German
17	Italian
19	Other (not A–Z)
	Congresses
21	International
22	American and English
23	French

25	German
27	Italian
29.A–Z	Other languages, A–Z
	Collected works (nonserial)
31	Several authors
33	Individual authors
35	Addresses, essays, lectures
	Dictionaries. Encyclopedias
40.A2	General works
40.A3–Z	Bilingual and polyglot
41	American and English
43	French
45	German
47	Italian
49.A–Z	Other languages, A–Z
49.5	Terminology. Abbreviations. Notation
50	Directories
	History
51	General works
53.A–Z	By region or country, A–Z
	Biography
57	Collective
59.A–Z	Individual, A–Z
	Theory. Method. Relation to other subjects
	Including social philosophy
61	General works
61.2	Classification
61.25	Mathematics. Mathematical models
61.26	Panel analysis
61.27	Scaling
61.28	Interviewing. Focused group interviewing
61.29	Biographical methods
61.3	Data processing

6.《國會圖書館分類大綱》(*L. C. Classification Outline*)

這是前述分類表的大綱。最新的一版是1990年出版的第六版。它把龐大的分類表簡化成43頁的綱領，其中包括40項大類分，三百餘項

小類分，以及它們所屬的類號範圍。對於國會圖書館分類制度不十分熟諳者，可以先從大綱著手。將整個大綱先瀏覽一遍，決定合適的類分及類號範圍。然後根據這些線索再從分類細表中找尋所需的正確類號，比直接從浩瀚的分類表卷帙中去搜索要來得方便並且可以避免謬誤。如果需要到藏書架中直接找尋某項主題，也可以攜帶大綱在手而按圖索驥。從教學上來說，師生各有大綱置於案前，綱舉目張，一目了然，極為便捷。大綱的形式見表10-5。

表10-5
POLITICAL SCIENCE

J	1 - 981	General legislative and executive papers
	(1 - 9)	Official gazettes
		The Library of Congress now classes this material in Class K
	10 - 87	United States documents
		For congressional hearings, reports, etc., *see* KF
	80 - 85	Presidents' messages and other executive documents
	86 - 87	State documents
	100 - 981	Other documents
		For documents issued by local governments, *see* JS
JA	1 - 98	Collections and general works
JC	11 - 628	Political theory. Theory of the state
	311 - 323	Nationalism
	325 - 341	Nature, entity, concept of the state
	345 - 347	Symbolism, emblems of the state: Arms, flag, seal, etc.
	348 - 497	Forms of the state
		Including imperialism, the world state, monarchy, aristocracy, democracy, fascism, dictatorships
	501 - 628	Purpose, functions, and relations of the state
	571 - 628	The state and individual. Individual rights. Liberty

			Constitutional history and administration
JF	8	-2112	General works. Comparative works
	201	- 723	Organs and functions of government
			Including executive branch, cabinet and ministerial government, legislative bodies
	751	- 786	Federal and state relations
	800	-1191	Political rights and guaranties
			Including citizenship, suffrage, electoral systems, representation, the ballot
	1321	-2112	Government. Administration
	2011	-2112	Political parties

			Special countries
JK	1	-9993	United States
	2403	-9501	State government
	9661	-9993	Confederate States of America

JL	1	-3899	British America. Latin America

JN	1	-9689	Europe

JQ	1	-6651	Asia. Africa. Australia. Oceania

JS	3	-8399	Local government
	141	- 231	Municipal government
	241	- 285	Local government other than municipal
	301	-1583	United States

7.《通用複分：字順索引》(*Free-Floating Subdivisions: An Alphabetical Index*)

目前使用的是2000年出版的第十二版。這本冊子依據字順(A–Z)排列所有的複分。告訴使用者每一個複分是在什麼場合使用，使用在什麼類別，那裡可以找到使用說明。對於編目者而言，這本冊子是最便利的參考手冊。例子請見表10–6。

表10-6

SUBDIVISION	FREE-FLOATING LIST IN SCM:SH	CATEGORY	USAGE GUIDELINES IN SCM:SH
-Hymns-History and criticism	H 1187	Christian denom	
◆ -Hymns-Texts	H 1187	Christian denom	
-Hypertrophy (*May Subd Geog*)	H 1164	Organs of body	
-Ice breaking operations	H 1159	Military srvces	
-Identification	H 1095	see SCM:SH	
	H 1100	Classes pers	
◆ -Identification	H 1147	Animals	
	H 1180	Plants & crops	
-Ideophone	H 1154	Languages	
-Idioms	H 1154	Languages	
-Ignition	H 1195	Land vehicles	
-Ignition-Electronic systems	H 1195	Land vehicles	
◆ -Illustrations	H 1095	see SCM:SH	H 1659
	H 1155.4	Indiv lit auth	H 1659
	H 1155.6	Lit works/Auth	H 1659
	H 1155.8	Lit works/Title	H 1659
	H 1156	Literatures	H 1659
	H 1188	Sacred works	H 1659
◆ -Illustrations-Catalogs	H 1155.4	Indiv lit auth	
◆ -Illustrations-Exhibitions	H 1155.4	Indiv lit auth	
-Imaging (*May Subd Geog*)	H 1150	Diseases	
	H 1164	Organs of body	
-Immunodiagnosis (*May Subd Geog*)	H 1150	Diseases	
-Immunological aspects	H 1150	Diseases	
-Immunology	H 1147	Animals	
	H 1149	Chemicals	
	H 1164	Organs of body	

◆ = *Form Subdivision*

二、備而待用的參考工具

除了上述的必備編目工具外，一個健全的編目室必需具備實用、周全，和權威性的參考書籍，以便隨時查閱。為了協助主題編目員充實他們的參考書籍，本節將主題編目處常用的參考書籍擇其要者，分列於以下四大類別之下：人文、科學、社會以及一般性的參考書籍❶，它們全屬英文的參考書籍。至於東方語文的參考書籍，國內典籍繁多，編目者皆耳熟能詳，毋庸贅述。

1.一般性參考書籍

The Columbia Lippincott Gazetteer of the World (New York: Columbia University Press, 1998)

New Encyclopedia Britannica (Chicago: Encyclopedia Britannica, 1998)

Encyclopedia International (New York: Lexicon Publications, 1982)

National Geographic Atlas of the World (Washington, D.C.: National Geographic Society, 1997)

The Oxford English Dictionary (New York: Oxford University Press, 1939–)

The Random House Dictionary of the English Language (New York: Random House, 1987)

Websters' New Geographical Dictionary (Springfield, Mass.: Merriam-Webster, 1988)

Webster's Third New International Dictionary of the English Lan-

---

❶ Library of Congress, *Subject Cataloging Manual: Subject Headings*, 5 th. ed. (Washington, D.C.: Library of Congress, 1996), H203, pp. 5–21.

guage, Unabridged (Springfield, Mass.: Merriam-Webster, 1993)

2.人文類參考書籍

Comprehensive Glossary of Psychiatry and Psychology (Baltimore: Williams & Wilkins, 1992)

A Dictionary of Comparative Religion (New York: Scribner's, 1987)

Dictionary of Language and Linguistics (London: Applied Science Publishers, 1972)

A Dictionary of Literary Terms (London: A. Deutsch, 1979)

The Encyclopedia Dictionary of Psychology (Cambridge, Mass.: MIT Press, 1983)

Encyclopedia Dictionary of Religion (Washington, D.C.: Corpus Publications, 1979)

Glossary of Linguistic Terminology (New York: Columbia University Press, 1966)

A Guide to The World's Languages (Stanford, Calif.: Stanford University Press, 1987–)

A Handbook of Literary Terms (Boston: H.L. Yelland, 1980)

Macmillan Encyclopedia of Architects (New York: Free Press, 1982)

McGraw-Hill Dictionary of Art (New York, McGraw-Hill, 1969)

The Penguin Dictionary of Architecture (New York: Penguin, 1991)

The Penguin Dictionary of Psychology (New York: Penguin Books, 1995)

Rutledge Encyclopedia of Philosophy (New York: Rutledge, 1998)

3.科學類參考書籍

Amphibian Species of the World: a Taxonomic and Geographical Reference (Lawrence, Kan., U.S.A.: Allen Press, 1985)

Black's Veterinary Dictionary (Totowa, N.J.: Barnes & Noble, 1988)

Blakiston's Gould Medical Dictionary: a modern comprehensive dictionary of the terms used in all branches of medicine and allied sciences (New York: McGraw-Hill, 1988)

Challinor's Dictionary of Geology (New York: Oxford University Press, 1986)

Checklist of the World's Birds: a complete list of the species, with names, authorities, and areas of distribution (New York: Quadrangle/New York Times Book Co., 1976)

Classification of Insects; Keys to the Living and Extinct Families of Insects and to the Living Families of Other Terrestrial Arthropods (Cambridge: The Museum, 1954)

A Complete Checklist of the Birds of the World (London: Macmillan, 1984)

Dictionary of Agriculture (Chicago: F. Dearborn, 1998)

Dictionary of Forestry in Five Languages (New York: Elsevier Pub. Co., 1966)

Jane's Dictionary of Military Terms (London: Macdonald and Jane's, 1975)

Encyclopedia of Computer Science (New York: Van Nostrand Reinhold Co., 1993)

Encyclopedia Dictionary of Mathematics (Cambridge, Mass.: MIT Press, 1993)

The Macmillan Dictionary of Astronomy (London: Macmillan Press, 1985)

Walker's Mammals of the World (Baltimore: Johns Hopkins University Press, 1999)

McGraw-Hill Dictionary of the Life Sciences (New York: McGraw-Hill, 1976)

McGraw-Hill Encyclopedia of Science and Technology: an international reference work in fifteen volumes including an index(New York: McGraw-Hill, 1997)

Medical and Health Related Sciences Thesaurus (Bethesda, Md.: U.S. Dept. of Health and Human Services, Public Health Service, National Institutes of Health, 1963–)

NASA Thesaurus (Washington, D.C.: National Aeronautics and Space Administration, Scientific and Technical Information Branch, 1985–)

Outline of Plant Classification (New York: Longman, 1983)

Psychiatric Dictionary (New York: Oxford University Press, 1996)

Stedman's Medical Dictionary (Baltimore: Williams & Wilkins, 1995)

Thesaurus of Scientific, Technical, and Engineering Terms (Cambridge, Mass.: Hemisphere Pub. Corp., 1988)

A World Dictionary of Livestock Breeds, Types and Varieties (Wallingford, Oxon: Commonwealth Agricultural Bureaux, 1996)

4.社會學類參考書籍

The American Political Dictionary (Fort Worth: Harcourt Brace, 1997)

Black's Law Dictionary: definitions of the terms and phrases of American and English jurisprudence, ancient and modern (St. Paul, Minn.: West Pub. Co., 1991)

The Blackwell Dictionary of Sociology (Malden, Mass: Blackwell, 1995)

Dictionary of Banking and Financial Services (New York: Wiley, 1985)

Dictionary of Business and Economics (New York: Free Press, 1986)

A Dictionary of Education (Sevenoaks, Kent: Hodder & Stoughton, 1993)

The Illustrated Encyclopedia of Mankind (New York: M. Cavendish, 1984)

International Dictionary of Education (Cambridge, Mass.: MIT Press, 1980)

The International Dictionary of Sports and Games (New York: Schocken Books, 1980)

International Encyclopedia of the Social Sciences (New York: Macmillan, 1979)

Macmillan Dictionary of Marketing & Advertising (New York: Nichols Pub. Co., 1990)

McGraw-Hill Dictionary of Modern Economics (New York: McGraw-Hill, 1984)

Outline of World Cultures (New Haven, Conn.: Human Relations Area Files, 1983)

The Penguin Dictionary of Sociology (New York: Penguin Books, 1994)

Reuters Glossary of International Financial & Economic Terms (Harlow, Essex: Longman, 1994)

The Stamp Collector's Encyclopedia (New York: Arco Pub. Co., 1973)

Thesaurus of International Trade Terms (Geneva: International Trade Centre UNCTAD/GATT, 1985)

Webster's Sports Dictionary (Springfield, Mass.: G. & C. Merriam, 1976)

參考書目

Angell, Richard S., *Standards for Subject Headings: A National Program,* Journal of Cataloging and Classification, 10: 193 (Oct. 1954).

Butler, Pierce, *An Introduction to Library Science,* Chicago: University of Chicago Press, 1933.

Chan, Lois Mai, *Library of Congress Subject Headings: Principles and Applications,* Littleton, Colo.: Libraries Unlimited, 3rd. ed. 1995.

Cutter, Charles A, *Rules for a Dictionary Catalog,* 4th. ed., Washington, D.C.: Government Printing Office, 1904.

Gail Sakurai, *Cornerstones of Freedom: The Library of Congress* (New York: Grolier Publishing, 1998)

Haykin, David Judson, *Subject Headings: A Practical Guide,* Washington, D.C.: Government Printing Office, 1951.

Library of Congress, *Guide to the Library of Congress,* Washington, D.C.: Library of Congress, 1985.

Library of Congress, *Free-Floating Subdivisions: An Alphabetical Index,* Washington, D.C.: Library of Congress, 1889–

Library of Congress, *Introducing LOCIS: MUMS,* Washington, D.C.: Library of Congress, 1987.

Library of Congress, *Library of Congress Information Bulletin,* Washington, D.C.: Library of Congress, June 27, 1983.

Library of Congress, *Library of Congress Information Bulletin,* Washington, D.C.: Library of Congress, Feb. 8, 1988.

Library of Congress, *The Library of Congress: Thomas Jefferson Building,* Washington D.C.: Library of Congress, 1997.

142 美國國會圖書館與主題編目

Library of Congress, Processing Services, *Statistical Highlights,* Washington, D.C.: Library of Congress, 1988.

Library of Congress, *Program for Cooperative Cataloging,* Washington, D.C.: LC Home Page, 1998.

Library of Congress, *Service to the Nation: The Library of Congress,* Washington, D.C.: Library of Congress, 1986.

Library of Congress, *Library of Congress Subject Headings,* Washington, D.C.: Library of Congress, 1975–

Library of Congress, Subject Cataloging Division, *Library of Congress Subject Headings; A Guide to Subdivision Practice,* Washington, D.C.: Library of Congress, 1981.

Library of Congress, *Subject Cataloging Manual: Subject Headings,* 5th. ed. Washington, D.C.: Library of Congress, 1996.

Library of Congress, Professional Association, *Automation at the Library of Congress: Inside Views,* Washington, D.C.: Library of Congress Professional Association, 1986.

Library of Congress, *25 Questions Most Frequently Asked by Visitors,* Washington D.C.: Library of Congress, 1997.

The Research Libraries Group, *RLG Chinese Aggregation Guidelines,* Stanford, Calif.: RLG, 1987.

Sukurai, Gail, *Cornerstones of Freedom: The Library of Congress,* New York: Grolier Publishing, 1998.

附錄一：模範標題下的複分
(Free-floating subdivisions under pattern headings)

1.宗教類(Religious and monastic orders)

(1)Jesuits

（註：形式複分之前有◆的標記）

◆－－Bio-bibliography

◆－－Controversial literature

　－－Customs and practices

　－－Education (*May Subd Geog*)

　－－Liturgy

◆－－Liturgy－－Texts

　－－Missions (*May Subd Geog*)

　－－Nazi persecution (*May Subd Geog*)

◆－－Necrology

　－－Occupations

◆－－Portraits

◆－－Prayer-books and devotions

◆－－Prayer-books and devotions－－English,〔French, German, etc.〕

　－－Prayer-books and devotions－－ History and criticism

◆－－Rules

　－－Spiritual life

　－－Theology

(2)Buddhism

♦ ‑‑Apologetic works

‑‑Apologetic works‑‑History and criticism

♦ ‑‑Catechisms

‑‑Charities

♦ ‑‑Controversial literature

‑‑Controversial literature‑‑History and criticism

♦ ‑‑Creeds

‑‑Customs and practices

‑‑Discipline

‑‑Doctrines

♦ ‑‑Doctrines‑‑Introductions

‑‑Essence, genius, nature

‑‑Government

‑‑Influence

‑‑Liturgical objects (*May Subd Geog*)

‑‑Missions (*May Subd Geog*)

‑‑Origin

‑‑Political aspects (*May Subd Geog*)

♦ ‑‑Prayer-books and devotions

♦ ‑‑Prayer-books and devotions‑‑ English, 〔French, German, etc.〕

‑‑Prayer-books and devotions‑‑ History and criticism

‑‑Psychology

‑‑Relations

‑‑Relations‑‑Christianity, 〔Islam, etc.〕

‑‑Rituals

♦ ‑‑Rituals‑‑Texts

♦ ‑‑Rituals‑‑Texts‑‑Concordances

　　--Rituals--Texts-- History and criticism

　　--Sacred books

　　--Sacred books--Hermeneutics

◆--Sacred books--Introductions

　　--Sacred books--Language, style

　　--Sacred books--Preservation

◆--Sacred books--Quotations

2.歷史和地理類(History and geography)

(1)Great Britain--Colonies

REGIONAL SUBDIVISIONS:

　　--Africa

　　--America

　　--Asia

　　--Oceania

　　--Administration

　　--Boundaries (*May Subd Geog*)

　　--Commerce (*May Subd Geog*)

　　--Defenses

　　--Description and travel

　　--Discovery and exploration

　　--Economic conditions

　　--Economic policy

　　--Emigration and immigration

　　--Geography

　　--History

　　--Officials and employees

　　--Population

--Race relations

--Religion

--Religious life and customs

--Rural conditions

--Social conditions

--Social life and customs

--Social policy

(2)**United States Congress**

--Alabama 〔Illinois, Texas, etc.〕 delegation

--Appropriations and expenditures

--Caucuses

--Censures

--Cloture

--Committees

♦--Committees--Indexes

--Committees--Rules and practice

--Committees--Seniority system

--Conference committees

--Constituent communication

--Contested elections

--Dissolution

--Election districts

--Elections

--Elections, 〔*date*〕

--Ethics

--Expulsion

--Facilities

  ——Food service

  ——Freedom of debate

  ——Leadership

  ——Majority leader

  ——Majority whip

  ——Minority leader

  ——Minority whip

  ——Officials and employees

  ——Officials and employees——Pensions

  ——Officials and employees——Salaries, etc.

  ——Pensions

  ——Powers and duties

  ——Presiding officer

♦——Private bills

  ——Privileges and immunities

  ——Publication of proceedings

  ——Qualifications

  ——Radio broadcasting of proceedings

  ——Reform

  ——Reporters and reporting

♦——Resolutions

  ——Salaries, etc.

  ——Speaker

  ——Television broadcasting of proceedings

  ——Term of office

  ——Voting

(3)**United States--History--Civil War, 1861-1865; World War, 1939-1945**

--Aerial operations

--Aerial operations, American, 〔British, etc.〕

--Afro-Americans

♦--Almanacs

--Amphibious operations

--Anniversaries, etc.

--Antiaircraft artillery operations

--Antiquities

--Armistices

♦--Art and the war, 〔revolution, etc.〕

--Artillery operations

--Artillery operations, American, 〔British, French, etc.〕

--Asian Americans

--Atrocities

♦--Autographs

--Balloons (*May Subd Geog*)

--Basques (*May Subd Geog*)

--Battlefields (*May Subd Geog*)

♦--Biography

--Biological warfare (*May Subd Geog*)

--Blacks (*May Subd Geog*)

--Blockades (*May Subd Geog*)

--Bomb reconnaissance

--Camouflage

--Campaigns (*May Subd Geog*)

--Cartography

--Casualties (*May Subd Geog*)

♦ ――Casualties――Statistics

――Causes

――Cavalry operations

――Censorship (*May Subd Geog*)

――Centennial celebrations, etc.

――Chaplains (*May Subd Geog*)

――Chemical warfare (*May Subd Geog*)

――Children (*May Subd Geog*)

♦ ――Chronology

――Civilian relief (*May Subd Geog*)

――Claims

――Collaborationists (*May Subd Geog*)

――Collectibles (*May Subd Geog*)

――Commando operations (*May Subd Geog*)

――Communications

――Concentration camps (*May Subd Geog*)

――Confiscations and contributions (*May Subd Geog*)

――Conscientious objectors (*May Subd Geog*)

――Conscript labor (*May Subd Geog*)

――Cossacks (*May Subd Geog*)

――Counterfeit money (*May Subd Geog*)

――Cryptography

――Desertions (*May Subd Geog*)

――Destruction and pillage (*May Subd Geog*)

――Diplomatic history

――Draft registers (*May Subd Geog*)

――Education and the war, 〔revolution, etc.〕

--Electronic intelligence (*May Subd Geog*)

--Engineering and construction

--Environmental aspects (*May Subd Geog*)

--Equipment and supplies

--Evacuation of civilians (*May Subd Geog*)

--Finance (*May Subd Geog*)

--Fire qighters (*May Subd Geog*)

--Flags

--Food supply (*May Subd Geog*)

--Forced repatriation

--Foreign public opinion

--Foreign public opinion, Austrian, 〔British, etc.〕

--Fuel supplies

--German Americans

◆--Gift books

--Governments in exile

--Graffiti

--Health aspects (*May Subd Geog*)

--Hospitals (*May Subd Geog*)

--In bookplates

--Indians

--Influence

--Italian Americans

--Japanese Americans

--Jews (*May Subd Geog*)

--Journalism, Military (*May Subd Geog*)

--Journalists

--Jungle warfare

--Language

--Law and legislation (*May Subd Geog*)

--Libraries

--Literature and the war, 〔revolution, etc.〕

--Logistics (*May Subd Geog*)

--Manpower (*May Subd Geog*)

--Mass media and the war, 〔revolution, etc.〕

--Medals (*May Subd Geog*)

--Medical care (*May Subd Geog*)

--Military currency (*May Subd Geog*)

--Military intelligence *May Subd Geog*)

--Missing in action (*May Subd Geog*)

--Monuments (*May Subd Geog*)

--Moral and ethical aspects (*May Subd Geog*)

--Motion pictures and the war, 〔revolution, etc.〕

--Museums (*May Subd Geog*)

--Music and the war, 〔revolution, etc.〕

--Name

--Naval operations

--Naval operations--Submarine

--Naval operations, American, 〔British, etc.〕

--Occupied territories

◆--Pamphlets

--Participation, Afro-American, 〔Indian, etc.〕

--Participation, Female

--Participation, Foreign

--Participation, German, 〔Irish, Swiss, etc.〕

--Participation, Immigrant

--Participation, Jewish

--Participation, Juvenile

--Peace

◆--Personal narratives

◆--Personal narratives, American, 〔French, etc.〕

◆--Personal narratives, Confederate

◆--Personal narratives, Jewish

--Photography

◆--Portraits

--Postal service

--Press coverage (*May Subd Geog*)

--Prisoners and prisons

--Prisoners and prisons, British, 〔German, etc.〕

--Prizes, etc.

--Propaganda

--Prophecies

--Protest movements (*May Subd Geog*)

--Protestant churches

--Psychological aspects

--Public opinion

--Radar

--Reconnaissance operations

--Reconnaissance operations, American, 〔German, etc.〕

--Refugees

--Regimental histories (*May Subd Geog*)

◆--Registers

◆--Registers of dead (*May Subd Geog*)

--Religious aspects

 Religious aspects--Baptists, 〔Catholic Church, etc.〕

 Religious aspects--Buddhism, 〔Christianity, etc.〕

--Reparations

--Riverine operations (*May Subd Geog*)

--Riverine operations, American, 〔British, etc.〕 (*May Subd Geog*)

--Science (*May Subd Geog*)

--Scouts and scouting

--Search and rescue operations (*May Subd Geog*)

--Secret Service (*May Subd Geog*)

◆--Sermons

--Social aspects (*May Subd Geog*)

 Songs and music

--Sounds

◆--Sources

--Tank warfare

--Technology

--Territorial questions (*May Subd Geog*)

--Theater and the war, 〔revolution, etc.〕

--Transportation (*May Subd Geog*)

◆--Treaties

--Trench warfare

--Trophies

--Tunnel warfare (*May Subd Geog*)

--Underground literature (*May Subd Geog*)

--Underground movements (*May Subd Geog*)

--Underground movements--Museums (*May Subd Geog*)

--Underground printing plants (*May Subd Geog*)

--Unknown military personnel

--Unknown military personnel, American, 〔British, etc.〕

--Veterans (*May Subd Geog*)

--Veterinary service (*May Subd Geog*)

--War work (*May Subd Geog*)

--War work--American Legion

--War work--Boy Scouts

--War work--Catholic Church, 〔Methodist Church, etc.〕

--War work--Churches

--War work--Elks

--War work--Girl Scouts

--War work--Red Cross

--War work--Salvation Army

--War work--Schools

--War work--Young Men's Christian Associations

--War work--Young Women's Christian Associations

--Women (*May Subd Geog*)

3.社會科學類(Social sciences)

(1)Construction industry; Retail trade

--Accidents (*May Subd Geog*)

--Accounting

--Accounting--Law and legislation (*May Subd Geog*)

--Appropriate technology (*May Subd Geog*)

--Auditing

--Automation

--Capital investments (*May Subd Geog*)

--Capital productivity (*May Subd Geog*)

--Certification (*May Subd Geog*)

--Communication systems

--Corrupt practices (*May Subd Geog*)

--Cost control

--Cost effectiveness

--Costs

--Credit ratings

--Customer services (*May Subd Geog*)

--Defense measures (*May Subd Geog*)

--Deregulation (*May Subd Geog*)

--Dust control (*May Subd Geog*)

--Econometric models

--Electric equipment (*May Subd Geog*)

--Electronic equipment

--Employees

--Employees--Diseases (*May Subd Geog*)

--Employees--Effect of technological innovations on (*May Subd Geog*)

--Employees--Health and hygiene (*May Subd Geog*)

--Employees--Legal status, laws, etc. (*May Subd Geog*)

--Employees--Medical care (*May Subd Geog*)

--Employees--Pensions (*May Subd Geog*)

--Employees--Pensions-- Law and legislation (*May Subd Geog*)

--Employees--Supply and demand (*May Subd Geog*)

--Employees--Training of (*May Subd Geog*)

--Energy conservation (*May Subd Geog*)

--Energy consumption (*May Subd Geog*)

--Environmental aspects (*May Subd Geog*)

--Equipment and supplies

--Estimates (*May Subd Geog*)

--Finance

--Finance--Law and legislation (*May Subd Geog*)

--Fires and fire prevention (*May Subd Geog*)

--Foreign ownership

--Fume control (*May Subd Geog*)

--Government ownership (*May Subd Geog*)

--Government policy (*May Subd Geog*)

--Health aspects (*May Subd Geog*)

--Industrial capacity (*May Subd Geog*)

--Information services

--Information services--Law and legislation (*May Subd Geog*)

--Insurance (*May Subd Geog*)

--Insurance--Law and legislation (*May Subd Geog*)

--Inventories

--Inventory control

--Labor productivity (*May Subd Geog*)

--Law and legislation (*May Subd Geog*)

--Licenses (*May Subd Geog*)

--Location (*May Subd Geog*)

--Management

--Management--Employee participation (*May Subd Geog*)

--Management--Employee participation--Law and legislation (*May Subd*

Geog)

--Materials management (*May Subd Geog*)

--Mergers (*May Subd Geog*)

--Military aspects (*May Subd Geog*)

--Noise

--Ownership

--Personnel management

--Planning

--Political activity

--Power supply (*May Subd Geog*)

--Prices (*May Subd Geog*)

--Prices--Government policy (*May Subd Geog*)

--Prices--Law and legislation (*May Subd Geog*)

--Production control (*May Subd Geog*)

--Production standards (*May Subd Geog*)

--Quality control

♦--Records and correspondence

--Safety measures

--Safety regulations (*May Subd Geog*)

--Sanitation (*May Subd Geog*)

--Seasonal variations (*May Subd Geog*)

--Security measures (*May Subd Geog*)

--Social aspects (*May Subd Geog*)

♦--Specifications (*May Subd Geog*)

--Standards (*May Subd Geog*)

--State supervision

--Statistical methods

--Statistical services

--Subcontracting (*May Subd Geog*)

--Taxation (*May Subd Geog*)

--Taxation--Law and legislation (*May Subd Geog*)

--Technological innovations (*May Subd Geog*)

♦--Telephone directories

♦--Trademarks

--Vertical integration (*May Subd Geog*)

--Vocational guidance (*May Subd Geog*)

--Waste disposal (*May Subd Geog*)

--Water-supply

(2)**Universities and colleges**

--Accounting

--Accreditation (*May Subd Geog*)

--Administration

--Admission

--Admission--Law and legislation (*May Subd Geog*)

--Alumni and alumnae (*May Subd Geog*)

♦--Archives

--Auditing

--Auditing--Law and legislation (*May Subd Geog*)

--Business management

♦--Chapel exercises

--Communication systems

--Communication systems--Contracting out (*May Subd Geog*)

--Corrupt practices (*May Subd Geog*)

♦--Curricula

--Decentralization (*May Subd Geog*)

--Departments

--Departments--Evaluation

--Elective system

--Employees

--Entrance examinations

--Entrance examinations--Law and legislation (*May Subd Geog*)

◆--Entrance examinations--Study guides

--Entrance requirements

--Evaluation

--Examinations

--Examinations--Law and legislation (*May Subd Geog*)

--Examinations-- 〔subject〕

--Faculty

--Finance

--Finance--Law and legislation (*May Subd Geog*)

--Food service (*May Subd Geog*)

--Graduate work

--Graduate work--Examinations

--Graduate work of women

--Graduation requirements

--Health promotion services (*May Subd Geog*)

--Honors courses (*May Subd Geog*)

--Insignia

--Law and legislation (*May Subd Geog*)

--Mergers (*May Subd Geog*)

--Names

--Open admission (*May Subd Geog*)

--Planning

♦--Prayers

--Privileges and immunities

--Public services

--Religion

--Residence requirements (*May Subd Geog*)

--Safety measures

--Sanitary affairs

♦--Sermons

--Services for (*May Subd Geog*)

--Services for--Contracting out (*May Subd Geog*)

--Sociological aspects

--Standards (*May Subd Geog*)

--Taxation (*May Subd Geog*)

--Taxation--Law and legislation (*May Subd Geog*)

(3)**Harvard University**

--Administration

--Admission

♦--Aerial views

--Alumni and alumnae (*May Subd Geog*)

--Bands

--Baseball

--Basketball

--Benefactors

--Buildings

--Buildings--Access for the physically handicapped

--Choral organizations

◆--Curricula

　--Degrees

　--Dissertations

　--Employees

　--Entrance examinations

　--Entrance requirements

　--Entrance requirements-- 〔subject〕

　--Examinations

　--Examinations-- 〔subject〕

　--Faculty

　--Finance

　--Football

　--Freshmen

　--Funds and scholarships

　--Golf

　--Graduate students

　--Graduate work

　--Hockey

　--Language

　--Mascots

　--Open admission

　--Orchestras

　--Parking

　--Public services

◆--Regulations

　--Riot, 〔*date*〕

--Riots

--Rowing

--Rugby football

--Sanitary affairs

--Sports

--Strike, 〔*date*〕

--Student housing

--Students

◆--Students--Yearbooks

--Swimming

--Tennis

--Track-athletics

--Volleyball

--Wrestling

(4)**Labor laws and legislation**

◆--Cases

--Codification

--Compliance costs (*May Subd Geog*)

--Criminal provisions

◆--Digests

◆--Forms

--Interpretation and construction

--Language

--Legal research

--Legislative history

◆--Popular works

--Research (*May Subd Geog*)

--Trial practice

4.文藝類(Arts)

(1)**Authors, English**

PERIOD SUBDIVISIONS:

--Old English, ca. 450-1100

--Middle English, 1100-1500

--Early modern, 1500-1700

--18th century

--19th century

--20th century

TOPICAL AND FORM SUBDIVISIONS:

--Aesthetics

◆--Chronology

--Journeys (*May Subd Geog*)

--Philosophy

--Political activity

--Political and social views

--Relations with men

--Relations with women

(2)**Shakespeare, William, 1564-1616. Hamlet**

--Criticism, Textual

◆--Illustrations

◆--Pictorial works

(3)**Beowulf (Literary Work)**

◆--Adaptations

--Appreciation (*May Subd Geog*)

--Authorship

--Characters

--Criticism, Textual

--Dramatic production

♦--Illustrations

--Language

♦--Language--Glossaries, etc.

♦--Parodies, imitations, etc.

--Style

♦--Translations

--Translations--History and criticism

♦--Translations into French, 〔German, etc.〕

--Translations into French, 〔German, etc.〕 --History and criticism

--Versification

(4)English language; French language; Romance languages

PERIOD SUBDIVISIONS:

(Period subdivisions established under English language.)

--Old English, ca. 450-1100

--Middle English, 1100-1500

--Early modern, 1500-1700

--18th century

--19th century

--20th century

TOPICAL AND FORM SUBDIVISIONS:

--Ability testing (*May Subd Geog*)

--Absolute constructions

--Accents and accentuation

--Acquisition

♦--Acronyms

--Address, Forms of

--Adjectivals

--Adjective

--Adverb

--Adverbials

--Affixes

--Agreement

--Alphabet

--Alphabet--Religious aspects

--Alphabet--Religious aspects--Buddhism, 〔Christianity, etc.〕

--Analogy

--Anaphora

--Animacy

--Apheresis

--Apposition

--Archaisms

--Article

--Aspect

--Aspiration

--Asyndeton

--Augment

--Auxiliary verbs

--Business English

--Capitalization

--Case

--Case grammar

--Cataphora

--Categorial grammar

--Causative

♦--Classification

--Classifiers

--Clauses

--Clitics

--Cognate words

--Cognate words--Dutch, 〔German, etc.〕

--Collective nouns

--Comparative clauses

--Comparison

--Complement

♦--Composition and exercises

--Compound words

--Computer-assisted instruction

--Computer-assisted instruction for foreign speakers

--Concessive clauses

--Conditionals

--Conjunctions

--Connectives

--Consonants

--Context

--Contraction

♦--Conversation and phrase books

♦--Conversation and phrase books--English

♦──Conversation and phrase books──French,〔Italian, etc.〕

♦──Conversation and phrase books──Polyglot

♦──Conversation and phrase books (for air pilots)

♦──Conversation and phrase books (for bank employees)

♦──Conversation and phrase books (for clergy, etc.)

♦──Conversation and phrase books (for construction industry employees)

♦──Conversation and phrase books (for domestics)

♦──Conversation and phrase books (for farmers)

♦──Conversation and phrase books (for fishers)

♦──Conversation and phrase books (for flight attendants)

♦──Conversation and phrase books (for gardeners)

♦──Conversation and phrase books (for geologists)

♦──Conversation and phrase books (for gourmets)

♦──Conversation and phrase books (for lawyers)

♦──Conversation and phrase books (for library employees)

♦──Conversation and phrase books (for mathematicians)

♦──Conversation and phrase books (for medical personnel)

♦──Conversation and phrase books (for merchants)

♦──Conversation and phrase books (for meteorologists)

♦──Conversation and phrase books (for museum employees)

♦──Conversation and phrase books (for musicians, musicologists, etc.)

♦──Conversation and phrase books (for petroleum workers)

♦──Conversation and phrase books (for police)

♦──Conversation and phrase books (for professionals)

♦──Conversation and phrase books (for restaurant and hotel personnel)

♦──Conversation and phrase books (for sailors)

♦──Conversation and phrase books (for school employees)

◆−−Conversation and phrase books (for secretaries)

◆−−Conversation and phrase books (for social workers)

◆−−Conversation and phrase books (for soldiers, etc.)

−−Coordinate constructions

−−Declension

−−Definiteness

−−Deixis

−−Deletion

−−Dependency grammar

−−Determiners

−−Diacritics

−−Dialectology

−−Dialects (***May Subd Geog***)

◆−−Dialects−−Glossaries, vocabularies, etc.

−−Dialects−−Grammar

−−Dialects−−Lexicology

−−Dialects−−Morphology

−−Dialects−−Phonetics

−−Dialects−−Phonology

−−Dialects−−Research (***May Subd Geog***)

−−Dialects−−Research−−Law and legislation (***May Subd Geog***)

−−Dialects−−Syntax

◆−−Dialects−−Texts

−−Diction

◆−−Dictionaries

◆−−Dictionaries−−Early works to 1700

◆−−Dictionaries−−French,〔Italian, etc.〕

◆－－Dictionaries－－Polyglot

◆－－Dictionaries, Juvenile

◆－－Dictionaries, Juvenile－－Hebrew, 〔Italian, etc.〕

　　－－Diminutives

　　－－Diphthongs

　　－－Direct object

　　－－Discourse analysis

　　－－Elision

　　－－Ellipsis

　　－－Emphasis

　　－－Enclitics

　　－－Epithets

　　－－Eponyms

　　－－Ergative constructions

　　－－Errors of usage

　　－－Etymology

　　－－Etymology－－Names

　　－－Euphemism

　　－－Exclamations

◆－－Exercises for dictation

　　－－Existential constructions

　　－－Figures of speech

◆－－Films for foreign speakers

◆－－Films for French, 〔Spanish, etc.〕 speakers

　　－－Foreign countries

　　－－Foreign elements

　　－－Foreign elements－－French, 〔Greek, Latin, etc.〕

--Foreign words and phrases

--Foreign words and phrases--Arabic, 〔Italian, etc.〕

--Function words

--Gallicisms

--Gemination

--Gender

--Gerund

--Gerundive

♦--Glossaries, vocabularies, etc.

♦--Glossaries, vocabularies, etc.--Polyglot

--Government

--Government jargon

--Gradation

--Grammar

♦--Grammar--Terminology

--Grammar--Theory, etc.

--Grammar, Comparative

--Grammar, Comparative--French, 〔Latin, etc.〕

--Grammar, Generative

--Grammar, Historical

--Grammatical categories

--Grammaticalization

--Graphemics

--Haplology

--Heteronyms

--Hiatus

--History

--Homonyms

--Honorific

--Ideophone

--Idioms

--Imperative

--Indeclinable words

--Indicative

--Indirect discourse

--Indirect object

--Infinitive

--Infixes

--Inflection

--Influence on foreign languages

--Influence on French, 〔Italian, etc.〕

--Intensification

--Interjections

--Interrogative

--Intonation

--Jargon

--Labiality

--Lexicography

--Lexicology

--Lexicology, Historical

--Locative constructions

--Machine translating

--Markedness

--Medical English

--Metonyms

--Metrics and rhythmics

--Mimetic words

--Modality

--Monosyllables

--Mood

--Morphemics

--Morphology

--Morphophonemics

--Mutation

--Mutual intelligibility

--Nasality

--Negatives

--Neutralization

--New words

--Nominals

--Noun

--Noun phrase

--Number

--Numerals

--Obscene words

--Obsolete words

--Onomatopoeic words

--Orthography and spelling

--Palatalization

--Paragraphs

--Parallelism

--Paraphrase

--Parenthetical constructions

--Paronyms

--Parsing

--Participle

--Particles

--Partitives

--Parts of speech

--Passive voice

--Pejoration

--Person

--Phonemics

◆--Phonetic transcriptions

--Phonetics

--Phonology

--Phonology, Comparative

--Phonology, Comparative--French, 〔German, etc.〕

--Phonology, Historical

--Phraseology

--Polysemy

--Possessives

--Postpositions

--Prepositional phrases

--Prepositions

--Pronoun

--Pronunciation

--Pronunciation by foreign speakers

--Prosodic analysis

--Provincialisms (*May Subd Geog*)

--Punctuation

--Quantifiers

--Quantity

◆--Readers

◆--Readers-- 〔topic〕

◆--Readers for new literates

--Reduplication

--Reference

--Reflexives

--Reform

--Relational grammar

--Relative clauses

--Religious aspects

--Religious aspects--Baptists, 〔Catholic Church, etc.〕

--Religious aspects--Buddhism, 〔Christianity, etc.〕

--Remedial teaching (*May Subd Geog*)

--Resultative constructions

◆--Reverse indexes

--Revival

--Rhetoric

--Rhyme

--Rhythm

--Roots

--Self-instruction

--Semantics

--Semantics, Historical

--Sentences

--Sex differences

--Slang

--Social aspects (*May Subd Geog*)

--Sonorants

♦--Sound recordings for foreign speakers

♦--Sound recordings for French, 〔Spanish, etc.〕 speakers

--Spectral analysis

--Spoken English (*May Subd Geog*)

--Spoken French, 〔Japanese, etc.〕 (*May Subd Geog*)

--Standardization

--Study and teaching (*May Subd Geog*)

--Study and teaching--Afro-American students

--Study and teaching--Bilingual method

--Study and teaching--Foreign speakers

--Study and teaching--Foreign speakers--Audio-visual aids

--Study and teaching--French, 〔Spanish, etc.〕 speakers

--Study and teaching--Immersion method

--Study and teaching (Continuing education) (*May Subd Geog*)

--Study and teaching (Continuing education)--Foreign speakers

--Study and teaching (Continuing education)--French, 〔Spanish, etc.〕 speakers

--Study and teaching (Early childhood) (*May Subd Geog*)

--Study and teaching (Early childhood)--Foreign speakers

--Study and teaching (Early childhood)--French, 〔Spanish, etc.〕 speakers

--Study and teaching (Elementary) (*May Subd Geog*)

--Study and teaching (Elementary)--Foreign speakers

--Study and teaching (Elementary)--French, 〔Spanish, etc.〕 speakers

--Study and teaching (Higher) (*May Subd Geog*)

--Study and teaching (Higher)--Foreign speakers

--Study and teaching (Higher)--French, 〔Spanish, etc.〕 speakers

--Study and teaching (Preschool) (*May Subd Geog*)

--Study and teaching (Preschool)--Foreign speakers

--Study and teaching (Preschool)--French, 〔Spanish, etc.〕 speakers

--Study and teaching (Primary) (*May Subd Geog*)

--Study and teaching (Primary)--Foreign speakers

--Study and teaching (Primary)--French, 〔Spanish, etc.〕 speakers

--Study and teaching (Secondary) (*May Subd Geog*)

--Study and teaching (Secondary)--Foreign

--Study and teaching (Secondary)--French, 〔Spanish, etc.〕 speakers

--Style

--Subjectless constructions

--Subjunctive

--Subordinate constructions

--Substitution

--Suffixes and prefixes

--Suppletion

--Switch-reference

--Syllabication

--Synonyms and antonyms

--Syntax

--Technical English

--Technical English--Translating into French, 〔German, etc.〕

　--Tempo

　--Temporal clauses

　--Temporal constructions

　--Tense

◆--Terms and phrases

　--Textbooks

◆--Textbooks for English, 〔French, etc.〕 speakers

◆--Textbooks for foreign speakers

◆--Textbooks for foreign speakers--English

◆--Textbooks for foreign speakers--German, 〔Italian, etc.〕

◆--Texts

　--Texts--Dating

　--Topic and comment

　--Transcription

　--Transitivity

　--Translating

　--Translating into French, 〔German, etc.〕

　--Transliteration

　--Transliteration into Korean, 〔Russian, etc.〕

　--Transmutation

　--Usage

　--Variation (***May Subd Geog***)

　--Verb

　--Verb phrase

　--Verbals

　--Versification

　--Vocabulary

--Vocalization

--Vocational guidance (*May Subd Geog*)

--Voice

--Vowel gradation

--Vowels

--Word formation

--Word frequency

--Word order

--Writing

--Written English

(5)English literature

I . *PERIOD SUBDIVISIONS:*

Literatures and genres, except drama:

--Old English, ca. 450-1100

--Middle English, 1100-1500

--Early modern, 1500-1700

--18th century

--19th century

--20th century

Drama:

--To 1500

--Early modern and Elizabethan, 1500-1600

--17th century

--Restoration, 1660-1700

--18th century

--19th century

--20th century

II. *AUTHOR GROUP SUBDIVISIONS:*

--Armenian authors

--Basque authors

--Black authors

--Buddhist authors

--Catalan authors

--Catholic authors

--Celtic authors

--Chinese authors

--Christian authors

--Christian Science authors

--Dravidian authors

--Druze authors

--European authors

--Foreign authors

--German authors

--Greek authors

--Hindu authors

--Irish authors

--Italian authors

--Jaina authors

--Japanese authors

--Jewish authors

--Korean authors

--Kyrgyz authors

--Lutheran authors

--Luxembourg authors

--Maori authors

--Maratha authors

--Men authors

--Mennonite authors

--Methodist authors

--Minority authors

--Mongolian authors

--Mormon authors

--Muslim authors

--Parsee authors

--Protestant authors

--Puritan authors

--Quaker authors

--Scottish authors

--Sindhi authors

--South Asian authors

--Swami-Narayani authors

--Turkish authors

--Ukrainian authors

--Untouchable authors

--Welsh authors

--White authors

--Women authors

--Yoruba authors

III. *TOPICAL AND FORM SUBDIVISIONS:*

♦ --Adaptations

--African influences

--American influences

--Appreciation (***May Subd Geog***)

--Arab influences

--Audio adaptations

◆--Bibliography

◆--Bibliography--First editions

--Brazilian influences

--Buddhist influences

--Celtic influences

--Censorship (***May Subd Geog***)

--Chinese influences

--Christian influences

◆--Chronology

--Classical influences

◆--Concordances

--Criticism, Textual

--Egyptian influences

--English influences

--European influences

--Explication

--Film and video adaptations

--Foreign countries

--Foreign countries--History and criticism

--Foreign influences

--French influences

--Galician influences

--German influences

--Greek influences

--History and criticism

--History and criticism--Theory, etc.

--Hungarian influences

♦--Illustrations

--Indic influences

--Iranian influences

--Irish influences

--Islamic influences

--Italian influences

--Japanese influences

--Latin American influences

--Manuscripts

--Mediterranean influences

--Memorizing

--Mexican influences

♦--Microform catalogs

--Minangkabau influences

♦--Musical settings

--Mycenaean influences

--Oriental influences

--Periodization

--Persian influences

--Polish influences

--Portuguese influences

--Publishing (*May Subd Geog*)

--Roman influences

--Russian influences

--Sanskrit influences

--Scandinavian influences

--Scottish influences

--Shamanistic influences

--Sources

--Spanish influences

♦--Stories, plots, etc.

--Taoist influences

--Themes, motives

♦--Translations

--Translations--History and criticism

♦--Translations into French, 〔German, etc.〕

--Translations into French, 〔German, etc.〕 --History and criticism

--Urdu influences

--West Indian influences

--Western influences

--Yiddish influences

(6)Operas

Period subdivisions.

--To 500

--500-1400

--15th century

--16th century

--17th century

--18th century

--19th century

--20th century

Form subdivisions for musical presentation and medium performance.

--2-harpsichord scores

--2-piano scores

--3-piano scores

--Chorus scores with piano

--Chorus scores without accompaniment

--Parts

--Parts (solo)

--Piano scores

--Piano scores (4 hands)

--Scores

--Scores and parts

--Scores and parts (solo)

--Solo with harpsichord

--Solo with harpsichord and piano

--Solo with keyboard instrument

--Solo with organ

--Solo with piano

--Solo with pianos (2)

--Solos with organ

--Solos with piano

--Solos with pianos (2)

--Vocal scores with accordion

--Vocal scores with continuo

--Vocal scores with guitar

--Vocal scores with harpsichord

--Vocal scores with keyboard instrument

--Vocal scores with organ

--Vocal scores with piano

--Vocal scores with piano (4 hands)

--Vocal scores with piano and organ

--Vocal scores with pianos (2)

--Vocal scores without accompaniment

--Cadenzas

--Excerpts

--Excerpts, Arranged

--Fake books

--Film and video adaptations

--Instructive editions

--Instrumental settings

--Lead sheets

--Librettos

--Scenarios

--Simplified editions

--Stage guides

--Teaching pieces

--Texts

Other free-floating subdivisions.

--Analysis, appreciation

♦--Bibliography

♦--Bibliography--Graded lists

♦--Discography

--Discography--Methodology

--First performances (*May Subd Geog*)

--History and criticism

◆--Instruction and study (*May Subd Geog*)

　--Interpretation (Phrasing, dynamics, etc.)

◆--Juvenile

◆--Juvenile--Instruction and study (*May Subd Geog*)

--Performances (*May Subd Geog*)

--Religious aspects

--Religious aspects--Baptists, 〔Catholic Church, etc.〕

--Religious aspects--Buddhism, 〔Christianity, etc.〕

◆--Stories, plots, etc.

◆--Thematic catalogs

--Themes, motives, literary

(7)Piano

◆--Catalogs, Manufacturers

◆--Catalogs and collections (*May Subd Geog*)

◆--Chord diagrams

--Construction (*May Subd Geog*)

--Customizing (*May Subd Geog*)

--Fingering

◆--Instruction and study (*May Subd Geog*)

◆--Instruction and study--Juvenile

◆--Methods

◆--Methods--Group instruction

◆--Methods--Juvenile

◆--Methods--Self-instruction

◆——Methods (Jazz, 〔Rock, Bluegrass, etc.〕)

　——Orchestra studies

　——Pedaling

　——Performance

　——Religious aspects

　——Religious aspects——Baptists, 〔Catholic Church, etc.〕

　——Religious aspects——Buddhism, 〔Christianity, etc.〕

◆——Studies and exercises

◆——Studies and exercises——Juvenile

◆——Studies and exercises (Jazz, 〔Rock, Bluegrass, etc.〕)

　——Tuning (*May Subd Geog*)

5.科學與技術類(Science and technology)

(1)Automobiles

　——Aerodynamics

　——Air conditioning (*May Subd Geog*)

　——Air disc brakes

　——Air suspension (*May Subd Geog*)

　——Anti-theft devices

　——Antilock brake systems

　——Audio equipment (*May Subd Geog*)

　——Automatic control

　——Axles

　——Batteries (*May Subd Geog*)

　——Bearings (*May Subd Geog*)

　——Bodies (*May Subd Geog*)

　——Bodies——Alignment (*May Subd Geog*)

　——Brakes

--Breaking in

--Bumpers

--Catalytic converters

--Chassis

--Climatic factors (*May Subd Geog*)

--Clutches

--Cold weather operation (*May Subd Geog*)

--Collectors and collecting (*May Subd Geog*)

--Collectors and collecting--Taxation (*May Subd Geog*)

--Collectors and collecting--Taxation--Law and legislation (*May Subd Geog*)

--Collision avoidance system (*May Subd Geog*)

--Collision damage (*May Subd Geog*)

--Conservation and restoration (*May Subd Geog*)

--Conservation and restoration--Taxation (*May Subd Geog*)

--Conservation and restoration--Taxation--Law and legislation (*May Subd Geog*)

--Corrosion (*May Subd Geog*)

--Cost of operation

--Crashworthiness (*May Subd Geog*)

--Customizing (*May Subd Geog*)

--Decoration (*May Subd Geog*)

--Defects (*May Subd Geog*)

--Defects--Law and legislation (*May Subd Geog*)

--Defects--Reporting (*May Subd Geog*)

--Design and construction

--Design and construction--Law and legislation (*May Subd Geog*)

--Design and construction--Optical methods

--Differentials

--Disc brakes

--Doors

--Dynamics

--Effect of environment on (*May Subd Geog*)

--Effect of explosive devices on (*May Subd Geog*)

--Electric equipment (*May Subd Geog*)

--Electric generators (*May Subd Geog*)

--Electric wiring

--Electronic equipment

--Environmental aspects (*May Subd Geog*)

--Equipment and supplies

--Fenders

--Fires and fire prevention (*May Subd Geog*)

--Front-wheel drive

--Fuel consumption

--Fuel consumption--Law and legislation (*May Subd Geog*)

--Fuel systems

--Fuel systems--Vapor lock

--Gas producers (*May Subd Geog*)

--Grilles

--Handling characteristics (*May Subd Geog*)

--Heating and ventilation (*May Subd Geog*)

--Horns

--Hydraulic equipment

--Ignition

--Ignition--Electronic systems

--Inspection (*May Subd Geog*)

--Instrument panels

--Instrument panels--Padding

--Instruments

--Instruments--Display systems

--Law and legislation (*May Subd Geog*)

--Licenses (*May Subd Geog*)

--Lighting (*May Subd Geog*)

--Lighting--Law and legislation (*May Subd Geog*)

--Locks

--Lubrication

--Maintenance and repair

--Maintenance and repair--Law and legislation (*May Subd Geog*)

--Maintenance and repair--Production standards (*May Subd Geog*)

--Marketing

--Materials

--Materials--Dynamic testing (*May Subd Geog*)

--Misfueling (*May Subd Geog*)

--Models (*May Subd Geog*)

--Models--Finishing (*May Subd Geog*)

--Models--Radio control (*May Subd Geog*)

--Motors

--Motors--Bearings (*May Subd Geog*)

--Motors--Camshafts

--Motors--Carburetors

--Motors--Combustion

--Motors--Computer control systems

--Motors--Control systems

--Motors--Cooling (*May Subd Geog*)

--Motors--Cooling systems (*May Subd Geog*)

--Motors--Crankshafts

--Motors--Cylinder blocks

--Motors--Cylinder heads (*May Subd Geog*)

--Motors--Cylinders

--Motors--Electronic fuel injection systems

--Motors--Exhaust gas

--Motors--Exhaust gas--Law and legislation (*May Subd Geog*)

--Motors--Exhaust systems

--Motors--Fuel injection systems

--Motors--Knock (*May Subd Geog*)

--Motors--Lubrication systems (*May Subd Geog*)

--Motors--Modification (*May Subd Geog*)

--Motors--Mufflers

--Motors--Mufflers--Acoustic properties (*May Subd Geog*)

--Motors--Oil filters

--Motors--Pistons and piston rings

--Motors--Soundproofing

--Motors--Superchargers

--Motors--Turbochargers

--Motors--Valves (*May Subd Geog*)

--Motors--Vibration (*May Subd Geog*)

--Motors (Compressed-gas)

--Motors (Diesel)

--Motors (Two-stroke cycle)

--Off road operation (*May Subd Geog*)

--Painting

--Parts

--Parts--Law and legislation (*May Subd Geog*)

--Performance

--Pneumatic equipment

--Pollution control devices

--Pollution control devices --Law and legislation (*May Subd Geog*)

--Power trains (*May Subd Geog*)

--Prices (*May Subd Geog*)

--Prices--Law and legislation (*May Subd Geog*)

--Protection (*May Subd Geog*)

--Radiator ornaments

--Radiators

--Radio equipment

--Radio equipment--Security measures (*May Subd Geog*)

--Registration and transfer (*May Subd Geog*)

--Retarders (*May Subd Geog*)

--Riding qualities (*May Subd Geog*)

--Safety appliances (*May Subd Geog*)

--Seat belts

--Seat belts--Law and legislation (*May Subd Geog*)

--Seats (*May Subd Geog*)

--Serial numbers

--Service life (*May Subd Geog*)

--Shock absorbers

--Sizes (*May Subd Geog*)

--Skidding (*May Subd Geog*)

--Snow protection and removal (*May Subd Geog*)

--Speed

--Spray control (*May Subd Geog*)

--Springs and suspension

--Stability

--Starting devices (*May Subd Geog*)

--Steering--gear

--Taxation (*May Subd Geog*)

--Taxation--Law and legislation (*May Subd Geog*)

--Tires

--Tires--Inflation pressure

--Tires--Repairing (*May Subd Geog*)

--Towing (*May Subd Geog*)

--Traction (*May Subd Geog*)

--Transaxles

--Transmission devices

--Transmission devices, Automatic

--Transmission devices, Automatic--Parts (*May Subd Geog*)

--Transportation (*May Subd Geog*)

--Transportation--Law and legislation (*May Subd Geog*)

--Upholstery (*May Subd Geog*)

--Vibration (*May Subd Geog*)

--Welding (*May Subd Geog*)

--Wheels

--Wheels--Alignment (*May Subd Geog*)

--Wheels--Balancing (*May Subd Geog*)

--Windows and windshields (*May Subd Geog*)

(2)**Copper; Insulin**

--Absorption and adsorption (*May Subd Geog*)

--Acoustic properties (*May Subd Geog*)

--Administration

--Affinity labeling (*May Subd Geog*)

--Agonists

--Allergenicity (*May Subd Geog*)

--Analysis

--Antagonists

--Assaying (*May Subd Geog*)

--Bioaccumulation (*May Subd Geog*)

--Bioavailability (*May Subd Geog*)

--Biodegradation (*May Subd Geog*)

--Biotechnology (*May Subd Geog*)

--Brazing (*May Subd Geog*)

--Brittleness

--Carcinogenicity (*May Subd Geog*)

--Cold working (*May Subd Geog*)

--Coloring

--Conformation (*May Subd Geog*)

--Controlled release (*May Subd Geog*)

--Corrosion (*May Subd Geog*)

--Creep (*May Subd Geog*)

--Decay

--Decontamination (*May Subd Geog*)

--Denaturation

--Density

--Derivatives (*May Subd Geog*)

--Design

--Diagnostic use (*May Subd Geog*)

--Diffusion rate

--Dipole moments

--Dose-response relationship

--Effect of radiation on (*May Subd Geog*)

--Effectiveness (*May Subd Geog*)

--Electric properties (*May Subd Geog*)

--Electrometallurgy

--Environmental aspects (*May Subd Geog*)

--Evolution (*May Subd Geog*)

--Excretion

--Fatigue

--Immunology

--Industrial applications (*May Subd Geog*)

--Inhibitors

--Isotopes

--Isotopes--Half-life

--Law and legislation (*May Subd Geog*)

--Lead content (*May Subd Geog*)

--Magnetic properties

--Mechanism of action

--Metabolic detoxication

--Metabolism

--Metabolism--Age factors (*May Subd Geog*)

--Metabolism--Disorders (*May Subd Geog*)

--Metabolism--Genetic aspects

--Metabolism--Regulation

--Metallography

--Metallurgy

--Methylation

--Molecular rotation

--Optical properties

--Oxidation (*May Subd Geog*)

--Pathophysiology

--Peroxidation

--Permeability

--Pharmacokinetics

--Physiological effect

--Physiological transport

--Prices (*May Subd Geog*)

--Psychotropic effects

--Purification (*May Subd Geog*)

--Quenching (*May Subd Geog*)

--Radioiodination

--Reactivity (*May Subd Geog*)

--Receptors

--Receptors--Effect of drugs on (*May Subd Geog*)

--Recycling (*May Subd Geog*)

--Sampling (*May Subd Geog*)

--Secretion

--Secretion--Regulation

--Separation

--Side effects (*May Subd Geog*)

--Solubility

--Speciation (*May Subd Geog*)

--Spectra

--Standards (*May Subd Geog*)

--Structure

--Structure-activity relationships

--Surfaces

--Synthesis

--Synthesis--Inhibitors

--Synthesis--Regulation

--Testing

--Therapeutic use (*May Subd Geog*)

--Therapeutic use--Administration

--Therapeutic use--Controlled release (*May Subd Geog*)

--Therapeutic use--Effectiveness (*May Subd Geog*)

--Therapeutic use--Side effects (*May Subd Geog*)

--Therapeutic use--Testing

--Thermal properties (*May Subd Geog*)

--Threshold limit values (*May Subd Geog*)

--Toxicity testing (*May Subd Geog*)

--Toxicology (*May Subd Geog*)

--Toxicology--Age factors (*May Subd Geog*)

♦--Toxicology--Biography

--Toxicology--Reporting (*May Subd Geog*)

--Viscosity (*May Subd Geog*)

--Welding (*May Subd Geog*)

(3)Cancer; Tuberculosis

--Adjuvant treatment (*May Subd Geog*)

--Age factors (*May Subd Geog*)

--Alternative treatment (*May Subd Geog*)

--Animal models (*May Subd Geog*)

--Chemoprevention (*May Subd Geog*)

--Chemotherapy (*May Subd Geog*)

--Chemotherapy--Complications (*May Subd Geog*)

--Chiropractic treatment (*May Subd Geog*)

--Complications (*May Subd Geog*)

--Cryosurgery (*May Subd Geog*)

--Cryotherapy (*May Subd Geog*)

--Cytodiagnosis (*May Subd Geog*)

--Cytopathology

--Diagnosis (*May Subd Geog*)

--Diet therapy (*May Subd Geog*)

♦ --Diet therapy--Recipes

--Differentiation therapy (*May Subd Geog*)

--Dosimetric treatment

--Eclectic treatment (*May Subd Geog*)

--Endocrine aspects

--Endoscopic surgery (*May Subd Geog*)

--Environmental aspects (*May Subd Geog*)

--Epidemiology

--Etiology

--Exercise therapy (*May Subd Geog*)

--Gene therapy (*May Subd Geog*)

--Genetic aspects

--Histopathology

--Homeopathic treatment (*May Subd Geog*)

--Hormone therapy (*May Subd Geog*)

--Hospitals (*May Subd Geog*)

--Imaging (*May Subd Geog*)

--Immunodiagnosis (*May Subd Geog*)

--Immunological aspects

--Immunotherapy (*May Subd Geog*)

--Interventional radiology (*May Subd Geog*)

--Intraoperative radiotherapy (*May Subd Geog*)

--Laser surgery (*May Subd Geog*)

--Law and legislation (*May Subd Geog*)

--Magnetic resonance imaging (*May Subd Geog*)

--Microbiology (*May Subd Geog*)

--Molecular aspects

--Molecular diagnosis (*May Subd Geog*)

--Mortality

--Nursing (*May Subd Geog*)

--Nutritional aspects

--Palliative treatment (*May Subd Geog*)

--Pathogenesis

--Pathophysiology

--Patients (*May Subd Geog*)

--Photochemotherapy (*May Subd Geog*)

--Physical therapy (*May Subd Geog*)

--Prevention

--Prognosis (*May Subd Geog*)

--Psychological aspects

--Psychosomatic aspects

--Radioimmunoimaging (*May Subd Geog*)

--Radioimmunotherapy (*May Subd Geog*)

--Radionuclide imaging (*May Subd Geog*)

--Radiotherapy (*May Subd Geog*)

--Radiotherapy--Complications (*May Subd Geog*)

--Relapse (*May Subd Geog*)

--Religious aspects

--Religious aspects--Baptists, 〔Catholic Church, etc.〕

--Religious aspects--Buddhism, 〔Christianity, etc.〕

--Reoperation (*May Subd Geog*)

--Reporting (*May Subd Geog*)

--Risk factors (*May Subd Geog*)

--Seasonal variations (*May Subd Geog*)

--Serodiagnosis

--Sex factors (*May Subd Geog*)

--Spectroscopic imaging (*May Subd Geog*)

--Surgery (*May Subd Geog*)

--Surgery--Complications (*May Subd Geog*)

--Surgery--Nursing (*May Subd Geog*)

--Susceptibility (*May Subd Geog*)

--Thermotherapy (*May Subd Geog*)

--Tomography

--Transmission (*May Subd Geog*)

--Treatment (*May Subd Geog*)

--Treatment--Complications (*May Subd Geog*)

--Ultrasonic imaging (*May Subd Geog*)

--Vaccination (*May Subd Geog*)

--Vaccination--Complications (*May Subd Geog*)

(4)**Fishes; Cattle**

--Abnormalities (*May Subd Geog*)

--Adaptation (*May Subd Geog*)

--Age

--Age determination

--Aging

--Anatomy

--Artificial insemination (*May Subd Geog*)

--Artificial spawning (*May Subd Geog*)

--Autopsy (*May Subd Geog*)

--Behavior (*May Subd Geog*)

--Behavior--Climatic factors (*May Subd Geog*)

--Behavior--Evolution (*May Subd Geog*)

♦--Biography

--Biological control (*May Subd Geog*)

--Breeding (*May Subd Geog*)

--Breeding--Selection indexes

--Buying

--Carcasses (*May Subd Geog*)

--Carcasses--Grading (*May Subd Geog*)

--Cardiovascular system

♦--Catalogs and collections (*May Subd Geog*)

♦ --Classification

--Climatic factors (*May Subd Geog*)

--Collection and preservation

--Color (*May Subd Geog*)

--Composition

--Condition scoring (*May Subd Geog*)

--Conformation (*May Subd Geog*)

--Control (*May Subd Geog*)

--Control--Environmental aspects (*May Subd Geog*)

--Control--Law and legislation (*May Subd Geog*)

--Cooperative marketing (*May Subd Geog*)

--Counting (*May Subd Geog*)

--Cultural control (*May Subd Geog*)

--Cytogenetics

--Cytology

--Development

--Digestive organs

--Diseases (*May Subd Geog*)

--Diseases--Alternative treatment (*May Subd Geog*)

--Diseases--Chemotherapy (*May Subd Geog*)

--Diseases--Diagnosis (*May Subd Geog*)

--Diseases--Diet therapy (*May Subd Geog*)

--Diseases--Epidemiology (*May Subd Geog*)

--Diseases--Genetic aspects

--Diseases--Nursing (*May Subd Geog*)

--Diseases--Nutritional aspects

--Diseases--Prevention

--Diseases--Treatment (*May Subd Geog*)

--Dispersal (*May Subd Geog*)

--Dissection (*May Subd Geog*)

--Ecology (*May Subd Geog*)

--Ecophysiology (*May Subd Geog*)

--Effect of chemicals on (*May Subd Geog*)

--Effect of cold on (*May Subd Geog*)

--Effect of dams on (*May Subd Geog*)

--Effect of drought on (*May Subd Geog*)

--Effect of drugs on (*May Subd Geog*)

--Effect of habitat modification on (*May Subd Geog*)

--Effect of heavy metals on (*May Subd Geog*)

--Effect of insecticides on (*May Subd Geog*)

--Effect of light on (*May Subd Geog*)

--Effect of logging on (*May Subd Geog*)

--Effect of metals on (*May Subd Geog*)

--Effect of noise on (*May Subd Geog*)

--Effect of oil spills on (*May Subd Geog*)

--Effect of pesticides on (*May Subd Geog*)

--Effect of pollution on (*May Subd Geog*)

--Effect of radiation on (*May Subd Geog*)

--Effect of salt on (*May Subd Geog*)

--Effect of sediments on (*May Subd Geog*)

--Effect of storms on (*May Subd Geog*)

--Effect of stray currents on (*May Subd Geog*)

--Effect of stress on (*May Subd Geog*)

--Effect of temperature on (*May Subd Geog*)

--Effect of volcanic eruptions on (*May Subd Geog*)

--Effect of water levels on (*May Subd Geog*)

--Effect of water pollution on (*May Subd Geog*)

--Effect of water quality on (*May Subd Geog*)

--Eggs (*May Subd Geog*)

--Eggs--Counting (*May Subd Geog*)

--Eggs--Incubation (*May Subd Geog*)

--Embryos

--Embryos--Anatomy

--Embryos--Physiology

--Embryos--Transplantation (*May Subd Geog*)

--Equipment and supplies

--Evolution (*May Subd Geog*)

--Exercise (*May Subd Geog*)

--Exercise--Physiological aspects

--Feed utilization efficiency (*May Subd Geog*)

--Feeding and feeds (*May Subd Geog*)

--Feeding and feeds--Climatic factors (*May Subd Geog*)

--Feeding and feeds--Equipment and supplies

--Fertility (*May Subd Geog*)

--Fetuses

--Fetuses--Anatomy

--Fetuses--Physiology

--Food (*May Subd Geog*)

--Fractures (*May Subd Geog*)

--Generative organs

--Genetic engineering (*May Subd Geog*)

--Genetics

--Genome mapping (*May Subd Geog*)

--Geographical distribution

--Germplasm resources (*May Subd Geog*)

--Germplasm resources--Cryopreservation (*May Subd Geog*)

--Germplasm resources--Microbiology (*May Subd Geog*)

--Grading (*May Subd Geog*)

--Grooming (*May Subd Geog*)

--Growth

--Habitat (*May Subd Geog*)

--Habitations (*May Subd Geog*)

--Handling (*May Subd Geog*)

--Health (*May Subd Geog*)

--Hibernation (*May Subd Geog*)

--Histology

--Histopathology

--Homing (*May Subd Geog*)

--Host plants (*May Subd Geog*)

--Housing (*May Subd Geog*)

--Housing--Air conditioning (*May Subd Geog*)

--Housing--Decoration (*May Subd Geog*)

--Housing--Design and construction

--Housing--Disinfection (*May Subd Geog*)

--Housing--Environmental engineering (*May Subd Geog*)

--Housing--Heating and ventilation (*May Subd Geog*)

--Housing--Insulation (*May Subd Geog*)

--Housing--Lighting (*May Subd Geog*)

--Housing--Odor control (*May Subd Geog*)

--Housing--Safety measures

--Housing--Sanitation (*May Subd Geog*)

♦ --Housing--Specifications (*May Subd Geog*)

--Housing--Waste disposal (*May Subd Geog*)

♦ --Identification

--Immunology

--Immunology--Genetic aspects

--Induced spawning (*May Subd Geog*)

--Infancy (*May Subd Geog*)

--Infections (*May Subd Geog*)

--Infertility (*May Subd Geog*)

--Inspection (*May Subd Geog*)

--Inspection--Risk assessment (*May Subd Geog*)

--Integrated control (*May Subd Geog*)

--Judging (*May Subd Geog*)

--Larvae (*May Subd Geog*)

--Larvae--Dispersal (*May Subd Geog*)

--Larvae--Ecology (*May Subd Geog*)

--Law and legislation (*May Subd Geog*)

--Life cycles (*May Subd Geog*)

--Locomotion

--Losses (*May Subd Geog*)

--Manure (*May Subd Geog*)

--Manure--Environmental aspects (*May Subd Geog*)

--Manure--Handling (*May Subd Geog*)

--Marketing

--Marketing--Law and legislation (*May Subd Geog*)

--Marking (*May Subd Geog*)

--Metabolism

--Metabolism--Climatic factors (*May Subd Geog*)

--Microbiology (*May Subd Geog*)

--Migration (*May Subd Geog*)

--Migration--Climatic factors (*May Subd Geog*)

--Molecular aspects

--Molecular genetics

--Monitoring (*May Subd Geog*)

--Morphogenesis (*May Subd Geog*)

--Morphology

--Mortality

--Mythology

--Names

--Nervous system

--Nests (*May Subd Geog*)

♦--Nomenclature

♦--Nomenclature (Popular)

--Nutrition

--Nutrition--Requirements

--Odor (*May Subd Geog*)

--Orientation (*May Subd Geog*)

--Origin

--Parasites (*May Subd Geog*)

--Parasites--Biological control (*May Subd Geog*)

--Parasites--Control (*May Subd Geog*)

--Parasites--Control--Environmental aspects (*May Subd Geog*)

♦--Parasites--Identification

--Parasites--Life cycles (*May Subd Geog*)

--Parturition (*May Subd Geog*)

--Pathogens (*May Subd Geog*)

♦--Pedigrees

♦--Performance records

--Phylogeny

--Physiology

--Pregnancy (*May Subd Geog*)

--Processing (*May Subd Geog*)

--Productivity (*May Subd Geog*)

--Psychic aspects (*May Subd Geog*)

--Psychological aspects

--Psychological testing (*May Subd Geog*)

--Psychology

--Quality

--Racial analysis (*May Subd Geog*)

--Religious aspects

--Religious aspects--Buddhism, 〔Christianity, etc.〕

--Reproduction

--Reproduction--Climatic factors (*May Subd Geog*)

--Reproduction--Endocrine aspects

--Reproduction--Regulation

--Respiration

--Respiratory organs

--Schooling

−−Seasonal distribution (*May Subd Geog*)

−−Selection

−−Sense organs

−−Services for (*May Subd Geog*)

−−Sexing (*May Subd Geog*)

−−Showing (*May Subd Geog*)

−−Size (*May Subd Geog*)

−−Spawning (*May Subd Geog*)

−−Speciation (*May Subd Geog*)

−−Speed

−−Spermatozoa

−−Spermatozoa−− Abnormalities (*May Subd Geog*)

−−Spermatozoa−−Morphology

−−Stranding (*May Subd Geog*)

−−Summering (*May Subd Geog*)

−−Surgery (*May Subd Geog*)

−−Surgery−−Complications (*May Subd Geog*)

−−Surgery−−Nursing (*May Subd Geog*)

−−Symbolic aspects (*May Subd Geog*)

−−Technological innovations (*May Subd Geog*)

−−Testing

−−Therapeutic use (*May Subd Geog*)

−−Toxicology (*May Subd Geog*)

−−Training (*May Subd Geog*)

−−Transportation (*May Subd Geog*)

−−Trypanotolerance (*May Subd Geog*)

−−Type specimens (*May Subd Geog*)

--Vaccination (*May Subd Geog*)

--Variation (*May Subd Geog*)

--Venom (*May Subd Geog*)

--Vertical distribution (*May Subd Geog*)

--Virus diseases (*May Subd Geog*)

--Viruses (*May Subd Geog*)

--Vocalization (*May Subd Geog*)

--Vocalization--Regulation

--Water requirements (*May Subd Geog*)

--Weight

--Wintering (*May Subd Geog*)

--Wounds and injuries (*May Subd Geog*)

附錄二：地區之下的複分
(Free-floating subdivisions under names of places)

--Abstracting and indexing (***May Subd Geog***)

♦ --Abstracts

--Administrative and political divisions

--Aerial exploration

♦ --Aerial photographs

♦ --Aerial views

--Altitudes

♦ --Anecdotes

--Annexation to...

--Anniversaries, etc.

--Antiquities

--Antiquities--Collection and preservation

--Antiquities, Byzantine

--Antiquities, Celtic

--Antiquities, Germanic

--Antiquities, Phoenician

--Antiquities, Roman

--Antiquities, Slavic

--Antiquities, Turkish

--Appropriations and expenditures

--Appropriations and expenditures --Effect of inflation on

　--Archival resources

　--Area

　--Armed Forces (***May Subd Geog***)

♦--Audiotape catalogs

♦--Bathymetric maps

♦--Bio-bibliography

♦--Biography

♦--Biography--Anecdotes

♦--Biography--Caricatures and cartoons

♦--Biography--Dictionaries

　--Biography--History and criticism

♦--Biography--Humor

♦--Biography--Pictorial works

♦--Biography--Portraits

♦--Book reviews

　--Boundaries (***May Subd Geog***)

　--Buildings, structures, etc.

♦--Calendars

　--Capital and capitol

♦--Census

　--Census--Law and legislation

♦--Census, 〔*date*〕

　--Centennial celebrations, etc.

♦--Charters

♦--Charters, grants, privileges

　--Church history

　--Church history--16th century

--Church history--17th century

--Church history--18th century

--Church history--19th century

--Church history--20th century

--Civilization

--Civilization--16th century

--Civilization--17th century

--Civilization--18th century

--Civilization--19th century

--Civilization--20th century

--Civilization--Foreign influences

--Civilization--Philosophy

--Claims

--Claims vs....

--Climate

◆--Climate--Observations

--Colonial influence

--Colonies

--Colonization

--Commerce (***May Subd Geog***)

--Commercial policy

◆--Commercial treaties

◆--Compact disc catalogs

◆--Constitution

◆--Constitution--Amendments

◆--Constitution--Amendments --1st, 〔2nd, 3rd, etc.〕

--Court and courtiers

--Court and courtiers--Costume

--Court and courtiers--Food

--Court and courtiers--Language

--Cultural policy

--Defenses

--Defenses--Economic aspects

--Defenses--Law and legislation

--Dependency on...

--Dependency on foreign countries

--Description and travel

♦--Directories

--Discovery and exploration

--Discovery and exploration--French, [Spanish, etc.]

--Distances, etc.

♦--Drama

♦--Early works to 1800

--Economic conditions

--Economic conditions--16th century

--Economic conditions--17th century

--Economic conditions--18th century

--Economic conditions--19th century

--Economic conditions--20th century

--Economic conditions-- [period subdivision, if established] --Regional disparities

--Economic conditions--Regional disparities

--Economic integration

--Economic policy

－－Emigration and immigration

－－Emigration and immigration－－Economic aspects

－－Emigration and immigration－－Government policy

－－Emigration and immigration－－Religious aspects

－－Emigration and immigration－－Religious aspects－－Baptists,　〔Catholic Church, etc.〕

－－Emigration and immigration－－Religious aspects－－Buddhism,　〔Christianity, etc.〕

－－Emigration and immigration－－Social aspects

－－Environmental conditions

－－Eruption,　〔*date*〕

－－Eruptions

－－Ethnic relations

－－Ethnic relations－－Economic aspects

－－Ethnic relations－－Political aspects

◆－－Fiction

◆－－Folklore

－－Forecasting

－－Foreign economic relations (***May Subd Geog***)

－－Foreign public opinion

－－Foreign public opinion, British,　〔French, Italian, etc.〕

－－Foreign relations (***May Subd Geog***)

－－Foreign relations－－Catholic Church

◆－－Foreign relations－－Executive agreements

－－Foreign relations－－Law and legislation

－－Foreign relations－－Philosophy

◆－－Foreign relations－－Treaties

--Foreign relations administration

♦--Gazetteers

♦--Genealogy

--Genealogy--Religious aspects

--Geography

--Gold discoveries

♦--Guidebooks

♦--Handbooks, manuals, etc.

--Historical geography

♦--Historical geography--Maps

--Historiography

--History

--History--16th century

--History--17th century

--History--18th century

--History--19th century

♦--History-- [period subdivision] --Biography

♦--History-- [period subdivision] --Biography--Anecdotes

♦--History-- [period subdivision] --Biography--Portraits

♦--History-- [period subdivision] --Chronology

--History-- [period subdivision] --Historiography

--History-- [period subdivision] --Philosophy

♦--History-- [period subdivision] --Sources

♦--History--Anecdotes

--History--Autonomy and independence movements

♦--History--Chronology

♦--History--Comic books, strips, etc.

--History--Errors, inventions, etc.

◆ --History--Humor

--History--Partition, 〔*date*〕

--History--Periodization

--History--Philosophy

◆ --History--Pictorial works

--History--Prophecies

--History--Religious aspects

--History--Religious aspects --Baptists, 〔Catholic Church, etc.〕

--History--Religious aspects --Buddhism, 〔Christianity, etc.〕

◆ --History--Sources

--History, Local

--History, Local--Collectibles

--History, Military

--History, Military--16th century

--History, Military--17th century

--History, Military--18th century

--History, Military--19th century

--History, Military--20th century

--History, Military--Religious aspects

--History, Naval

--History, Naval--16th century

--History, Naval--17th century

--History, Naval--18th century

--History, Naval--19th century

--History, Naval--20th century

◆ --Humor

♦ --Imprints

--In art

--In literature

--In mass media

--In motion pictures

♦ --Index maps

--Information services

--Intellectual life

--Intellectual life--16th century

--Intellectual life--17th century

--Intellectual life--18th century

--Intellectual life--19th century

--Intellectual life--20th century

--International status

♦ --Juvenile drama

♦ --Juvenile fiction

♦ --Juvenile humor

♦ --Juvenile poetry

--Kings and rulers

--Kings and rulers--Art patronage

--Kings and rulers--Brothers

--Kings and rulers--Children

--Kings and rulers--Death and burial

--Kings and rulers--Dwellings

--Kings and rulers--Education

♦ --Kings and rulers--Folklore

♦ --Kings and rulers--Genealogy

--Kings and rulers--Heraldry

--Kings and rulers--Journeys

--Kings and rulers--Mistresses

--Kings and rulers--Mothers

--Kings and rulers--Mythology

--Kings and rulers--Religious aspects

--Kings and rulers--Sisters

--Kings and rulers--Succession

--Kings and rulers--Tombs

--Languages

--Languages--Law and legislation

--Languages--Political aspects

◆--Languages--Texts

--Library resources

◆--Literary collections

◆--Literatures

--Manufactures

◆--Maps

◆--Maps--Bibliography

◆--Maps--Early works to 1800

◆--Maps--Facsimiles

◆--Maps, Comparative

◆--Maps, Manuscript

◆--Maps, Mental

◆--Maps, Outline and base

◆--Maps, Physical

◆--Maps, Pictorial

♦ -- Maps, Topographic

♦ -- Maps, Tourist

♦ -- Maps for children

♦ -- Maps for the blind

♦ -- Maps for the visually handicapped

-- Military policy

-- Military policy -- Religious aspects

-- Military relations (***May Subd Geog***)

-- Military relations -- Foreign countries

-- Militia

♦ -- Miscellanea

-- Moral conditions

-- Name

-- National Guard

-- Naval militia

♦ -- Newspapers

-- Officials and employees (***May Subd Geog***)

-- Officials and employees -- Accidents (***May Subd Geog***)

-- Officials and employees -- Foreign countries

-- Officials and employees -- Foreign countries -- Foreign language competency

-- Officials and employees -- Furloughs

♦ -- Officials and employees -- Leave regulations

-- Officials and employees -- Payroll deductions

-- Officials and employees -- Salaries, etc. (***May Subd Geog***)

-- Officials and employees -- Salaries, etc. -- Regional disparities

-- Officials and employees -- Turnover

-- Officials and employees, Alien

--Officials and employees, Honorary

--Officials and employees, Retired

--On postage stamps

◆--Photographs from space

◆--Pictorial works

◆--Poetry

--Politics and government

--Politics and government--16th century

--Politics and government--17th century

--Politics and government--18th century

--Politics and government--19th century

--Politics and government--20th century

--Politics and government -- 〔period subdivision〕 --Philosophy

--Politics and government--Philosophy

--Population

--Population--Economic aspects

--Population policy

◆--Posters

◆--Quotations, maxims, etc.

--Race relations

--Race relations--Economic aspects

--Race relations--Political aspects

◆--Registers

--Relations (***May Subd Geog***)

--Relations--Foreign countries

◆--Relief models

--Religion

　--Religion--16th century

　--Religion--17th century

　--Religion--18th century

　--Religion--19th century

　--Religion--20th century

　--Religion--Economic aspects

　--Religious life and customs

◆--Remote-sensing images

◆--Remote-sensing maps

　--Research (*May Subd Geog*)

　--Rural conditions

　--Seal

◆--Slides

　--Social conditions

　--Social conditions--16th century

　--Social conditions--17th century

　--Social conditions--18th century

　--Social conditions--19th century

　--Social conditions--20th century

　--Social life and customs

　--Social life and customs--16th century

　--Social life and customs--17th century

　--Social life and customs--18th century

　--Social life and customs--19th century

　--Social life and customs--20th century

　--Social policy

◆--Songs and music

　　--Statistical services

　　--Statistical services--Law and legislation

◆--Statistics

◆--Statistics, Medical

◆--Statistics, Vital

　　--Strategic aspects

　　--Study and teaching (*May Subd Geog*)

　　--Study and teaching-- Law and legislation (*May Subd Geog*)

◆--Surveys

◆--Telephone directories

◆--Telephone directories--Yellow pages

　　--Territorial expansion

　　--Territories and possessions

◆--Tours

◆--Trials, litigation, etc.

Also free-floating:

　　...Metropolitan Area (〔geographic qualifier〕)

　　...Suburban Area (〔geographic qualifier〕)

　　...Region (〔geographic qualifier〕)

附錄三： 水源之下的複分
(Free-floating subdivisions under bodies of water)

--Alluvial plain

--Channelization

--Channels

--Fertilization

--Navigation

--Navigation--Law and legislation

--Power utilization

--Recreational use

--Regulation

--Water rights

附錄四：個人名稱之下的複分
(Free-floating subdivisions under names of persons)

——Abdication, 〔*date*〕

♦——Abstracts

    Acting, see ——Dramatic production; ——Stage history

♦——Adaptations

  ——Adversaries

  ——Aesthetics

  ——Alcohol use

  ——Allusions

♦——Anecdotes

  ——Anniversaries, etc.

  ——Anonyms and synonyms

  ——Appreciation (***May Subd Geog***)

  ——Archaeological collections

♦——Archives

♦——Art

  ——Art collections

  ——Art patronage

  ——Assassination

  ——Assassination attempt, 〔*date*〕

  ——Assassination attempts

♦——Audio adaptations

♦ −−Audiotape catalogs

−−Authorship

−−Authorship−−Collaboration

♦ −−Autographs

−−Awards

♦ −−Bibliography

♦ −−Bibliography−−First editions

−−Birth

−−Birthplace

−−Bonsai collections

−−Books and reading

♦ −−Calendars

−−Captivity, 〔*dates*〕

−−Career in 〔specific field or discipline〕

♦ −−Caricatures and cartoons

♦ −−Catalogs

♦ −−Catalogues raisonnés

−−Censorship (*May Subd Geog*)

−−Characters

−−Characters−−Children, 〔Jews, Physicians, etc.〕

−−Characters−− 〔name of individual character〕

−−Childhood and youth

♦ −−Chronology

−−Cipher

−−Claims vs ....

−−Clothing

−−Coin collections

　--Collectibles (*May Subd Geog*)

　--Comedies

◆--Comic books, strips, etc.

◆--Compact disc catalogs

◆--Concordances

　--Contemporaries

　--Contributions in 〔specific field or topic〕

　--Coronation

◆--Correspondence

◆--Correspondence--Microform catalogs

　--Criticism, Textual

　--Criticism and interpretation

　--Criticism and interpretation--History

　--Criticism and interpretation--History--16th century

　--Criticism and interpretation--History--17th century

　--Criticism and interpretation--History--18th century

　--Criticism and interpretation--History--19th century

　--Criticism and interpretation--History--20th century

　--Cult (*May Subd Geog*)

　--Death and burial

　--Death mask

◆--Diaries

　--Disciples

◆--Discography

　--Divorce

◆--Drama

　--Dramatic production

--Dramatic works

--Dramaturgy

--Drug use

--Employees

--Estate

--Ethics

--Ethnological collections

--Ethnomusicological collections

--Exile (*May Subd Geog*)

--Family

♦--Fiction

--Fictional works

♦--Film and video adaptations

--Finance, Personal

--Forgeries (*May Subd Geog*)

--Freemasonry

--Friends and associates

--Hadith

--Harmony

--Health

--Herbarium

--Homes and haunts (*May Subd Geog*)

♦--Humor

♦--Illustrations

--Impeachment

--Imprisonment

--In bookplates

--In literature

--In mass media

--In motion pictures

--Inauguration, 〔*date*〕

--Influence

--Information services

◆--Interviews

--Journeys (***May Subd Geog***)

◆--Juvenile drama

◆--Juvenile fiction

◆--Juvenile humor

◆--Juvenile poetry

--Kidnapping, 〔*date*〕

--Knowledge--Agriculture, 〔America, etc.〕

--Knowledge and learning

--Language

◆--Language--Glossaries, etc.

--Last years

◆--Legends

--Library

◆--Library--Marginal notes

◆--Library--Microform catalogs

--Library resources

--Literary art

◆--Literary collections

--Literary style

--Manuscripts

- --Map collections
- --Marriage
- --Medals
- ◆ --Meditations
- --Mental health
- --Military leadership
- ◆ --Miscellanea
- --Monuments (*May Subd Geog*)
- --Motion picture plays
- --Museums (*May Subd Geog*)
- --Musical instrument collections
- ◆ --Musical settings
- --Musical settings--History and criticism
- --Name
- --Natural history collections
- ◆ --Notebooks, sketchbooks, etc.
- --Numismatic collections
- --Numismatics
- --On postage stamps
- --Oratory
- ◆ --Outlines, syllabi, etc.
- --Palaces
- --Pardon
- ◆ --Parodies, imitations, etc.
- --Performances (*May Subd Geog*)
- --Philosophy
- --Photograph collections

◆ーーPictorial works

　ーーPoetic works

◆ーーPoetry

　ーーPolitical activity

　ーーPolitical and social views

◆ーーPortraits

　ーーPoster collections

◆ーーPosters

◆ーーPrayer-books and devotions

◆ーーPrayer-books and devotions——English, 〔French, German, etc.〕

　ーーPrayer-books and devotions——History and criticism

　ーーPre-existence

　ーーProphecies

　ーーProse

　ーーPsychology

　ーーPublic opinion

◆ーーQuotations

　ーーRadio and television plays

　ーーRelations with 〔specific class of persons or ethnic group〕

　ーーRelations with men

　ーーRelations with women

　ーーRelics (***May Subd Geog***)

　ーーReligion

　ーーResignation from office

◆ーーRomances

◆ーーScholia

　ーーScientific apparatus collections

--Seal

♦ --Self-portraits

♦ --Sermons

--Settings

--Sexual behavior

--Shrines (*May Subd Geog*)

--Slide collections

♦ --Slides

--Societies, etc.

♦ --Songs and music

--Sources

--Spiritualistic interpretations

--Spurious and doubtful works

--Stage history (*May Subd Geog*)

--Stamp collections

--Statues (*May Subd Geog*)

♦ --Stories, plots, etc.

--Symbolism

--Teachings

--Technique

♦ --Thematic catalogs

--Themes, motives

--Titles

--Tomb

--Tragedies

--Tragicomedies

♦ --Translations

--Translations--History and criticism

◆--Translations into French, 〔German, etc.〕

　--Translations into French, 〔German, etc.〕 --History and criticism

◆--Trials, litigation, etc.

　--Versification

　--Views on 〔specific topic〕

　--Will

　--Written works

附錄五：機關名稱之下的複分
(Free-floating subdivisions under corporate bodies)

♦ --Abstracts

--Accounting

--Accreditation (*May Subd Geog*)

--Administration

♦ --Anecdotes

--Anniversaries, etc.

--Appropriations and expenditures

--Appropriations and expenditures--Effect of inflation on

--Archaeological collections

♦ --Archives

--Art collections

--Art patronage

♦ --Audiotape catalogs

--Auditing

--Automation

--Awards

♦ --Bibliography

♦ --Biography

♦ --Biography Dictionaries

--Biography--History and criticism

♦ --Biography--Portraits

　--Bonsai collections

　--Buildings

◆--By-laws

◆--Calendars

◆--Caricatures and cartoons

◆--Case studies

◆--Catalogs

　--Centennial celebrations, etc.

　--Chaplains

　--Charities

◆--Charters

　--Claims vs ....

　--Coin collections

　--Collectibles (**May Subd Geog**)

◆--Comic books, strips, etc.

　--Communication systems

◆--Compact disc catalogs

◆--Constitution

　--Corrupt practices

　--Customer services

　--Data processing

　--Decision making

◆--Directories

　--Discipline

◆--Discography

◆--Drama

　--Elections

－－Employees

－－Endowments

－－Equipment and supplies

－－Ethnological collections

－－Ethnomusicological collections

－－Evaluation

－－Examinations

－－Explosion,〔*date*〕

◆－－Fiction

－－Finance

－－Fire,〔*date*〕

◆－－Forms

◆－－Genealogy

◆－－Guidebooks

－－Heraldry

－－Herbarium

－－Historiography

－－History

－－History－－16th century

－－History－－17th century

－－History－－18th century

－－History－－19th century

－－History－－20th century

◆－－History－－Chronology

◆－－History－－Sources

－－Homes and haunts (***May Subd Geog***)

◆－－Humor

　　--In art

　　--In bookplates

　　--In literature

　　--In mass media

　　--In motion pictures

♦--Indexes

　　--Influence

　　--Information services

　　--Insignia

♦--Interviews

　　--Inventory control

♦--Job descriptions

♦--Juvenile drama

♦--Juvenile fiction

♦--Juvenile humor

♦--Juvenile poetry

　　--Language

　　--Libraries

　　--Library

　　--Library resources

♦--Literary collections

　　--Management

　　--Map collections

♦--Maps

♦--Maps--Bibliography

♦--Maps for children

　　--Medals

--Membership

♦--Microform catalogs

♦--Miscellanea

--Museums

--Musical instrument collections

--Name

--Natural history collections

--Numismatic collections

--Officials and employees

--Officials and employees--Accidents

--Officials and employees--Furloughs

♦--Officials and employees--Leave regulations

--Officials and employees--Salaries, etc.

--Officials and employees--Salaries, etc.--Regional disparities

--Officials and employees--Turnover

--On postage stamps

--Organ

--Organs

--Party work

--Performances (*May Subd Geog*)

--Personnel management

--Personnel records

--Photograph collections

♦--Pictorial works

--Planning

♦--Platforms

♦--Poetry

--Political activity

--Positions

--Poster collections

♦ --Posters

--Presidents

--Press coverage

--Privileges and immunities

--Procurement

--Public opinion

--Public records

--Public relations (*May Subd Geog*)

--Publishing (*May Subd Geog*)

--Purges

♦ --Records and correspondence

♦ --Registers

--Religion

--Reorganization

--Research (*May Subd Geog*)

--Research grants

--Rituals

♦ --Rules and practice

--Sanitation

--Scientific apparatus collections

--Seal

--Security measures

--Slide collections

--Societies, etc.

♦ --Songs and music

　--Stamp collections

♦ --Statistics

♦ --Telephone directories

♦ --Terminology

♦ --Trials, litigation, etc.

　--Uniforms

　--Vocational guidance (*May Subd Geog*)

附錄六：種族名稱之下的複分
(Free-floating subdivisions under ethnic groups)

--Abstracting and indexing (*May Subd Geog*)

♦--Abstracts

--Agriculture (*May Subd Geog*)

--Alcohol use (*May Subd Geog*)

♦--Anecdotes

--Anniversaries, etc.

--Anthropometry (*May Subd Geog*)

--Antiquities

--Antiquities--Collection and preservation

--Antiquities--Collectors and collecting (*May Subd Geog*)

--Antiquities--Private collections (*May Subd Geog*)

♦--Archives

--Assaults against (*May Subd Geog*)

--Attitudes

♦--Audiotape catalogs

♦--Autographs

♦--Bio-bibliography

♦--Biography

♦--Biography--Dictionaries

--Biography--History and criticism

--Boats (*May Subd Geog*)

◆--Book reviews

◆--Books and reading (*May Subd Geog*)

◆--Caricatures and cartoons

◆--Case studies

◆--Census

◆--Census, 〔*date*〕

--Charitable contributions (*May Subd Geog*)

--Charities

--Civil rights (*May Subd Geog*)

--Claims

--Collectibles (*May Subd Geog*)

--Colonization (*May Subd Geog*)

◆--Comic books, strips, etc.

--Commerce (*May Subd Geog*)

--Communication

◆--Correspondence

--Costume (*May Subd Geog*)

--Counseling of (*May Subd Geog*)

--Craniology (*May Subd Geog*)

--Crimes against (*May Subd Geog*)

--Cultural assimilation (*May Subd Geog*)

--Death

--Dental care (*May Subd Geog*)

◆--Diaries

◆--Dictionaries

◆--Directories

◆--Discography

--Diseases (*May Subd Geog*)

--Domestic animals (*May Subd Geog*)

♦--Drama

--Drug use (*May Subd Geog*)

--Dwellings (*May Subd Geog*)

♦--Early works to 1800

--Economic conditions

--Economic conditions--16th century

--Economic conditions--17th century

--Economic conditions--18th century

--Economic conditions--19th century

--Economic conditions--20th century

--Education (*May Subd Geog*)

--Education--Law and legislation (*May Subd Geog*)

--Education (Continuing education) (*May Subd Geog*)

--Education (Early childhood) (*May Subd Geog*)

--Education (Elementary) (*May Subd Geog*)

--Education (Graduate) (*May Subd Geog*)

--Education (Higher) (*May Subd Geog*)

--Education (Middle school) (*May Subd Geog*)

--Education (Preschool) (*May Subd Geog*)

--Education (Primary) (*May Subd Geog*)

--Education (Secondary) (*May Subd Geog*)

--Employment (*May Subd Geog*)

--Employment--Foreign countries

--Ethnic identity

　　　Do not use under Jews. Use Jews--Identity instead.

--Ethnobiology (*May Subd Geog*)

--Ethnobotany (*May Subd Geog*)

--Ethnozoology (*May Subd Geog*)

◆--Examinations, questions, etc.

◆--Fiction

--Finance

--Finance--Law and legislation (*May Subd Geog*)

--Finance, Personal

--Fishing (*May Subd Geog*)

◆--Folklore

--Food (*May Subd Geog*)

--Foreign countries

--Foreign influences

--Funeral customs and rites (*May Subd Geog*)

--Gambling (*May Subd Geog*)

--Games (*May Subd Geog*)

◆--Genealogy

--Government policy (*May Subd Geog*)

--Government relations

--Health and hygiene (*May Subd Geog*)

--Historiography

--History

--History--16th century

--History--17th century

--History--18th century

--History--19th century

--History--20th century

♦ーーHistory--Chronology

♦ーーHistory--Sources

　ーーHome care (*May Subd Geog*)

　ーーHomes and haunts (*May Subd Geog*)

　ーーHospice care (*May Subd Geog*)

　ーーHospital care (*May Subd Geog*)

　ーーHospitals (*May Subd Geog*)

　ーーHousing (*May Subd Geog*)

♦ーーHumor

　ーーHunting (*May Subd Geog*)

　ーーImplements (*May Subd Geog*)

　ーーIndustries (*May Subd Geog*)

　ーーInformation services

　ーーInstitutional care (*May Subd Geog*)

　ーーIntellectual life

　ーーIntellectual life--16th century

　ーーIntellectual life--17th century

　ーーIntellectual life--18th century

　ーーIntellectual life--19th century

　ーーIntellectual life--20th century

　ーーIntelligence levels (*May Subd Geog*)

　ーーIntelligence testing (*May Subd Geog*)

♦ーーInterviews

　ーーJewelry (*May Subd Geog*)

　ーーJob stress (*May Subd Geog*)

♦ーーJuvenile drama

♦ーーJuvenile fiction

◆ --Juvenile humor

◆ --Juvenile poetry

--Kings and rulers

--Kings and rulers--Children

--Kings and rulers--Education

◆ --Kings and rulers--Folklore

◆ --Kings and rulers--Genealogy

--Kings and rulers--Mythology

--Kings and rulers--Religious aspects

--Kings and rulers--Succession

--Kinship (*May Subd Geog*)

--Land tenure (*May Subd Geog*)

--Languages

◆ --Languages--Texts

--Legal status, laws, etc. (*May Subd Geog*)

--Library resources

◆ --Life skills guides

◆ --Literary collections

◆ --Longitudinal studies

--Manuscripts

◆ --Maps

--Marriage customs and rites (*May Subd Geog*)

--Material culture (*May Subd Geog*)

--Mathematics

--Medals (*May Subd Geog*)

--Medical care (*May Subd Geog*)

--Medical examinations (*May Subd Geog*)

--Medicine (*May Subd Geog*)

--Mental health (*May Subd Geog*)

--Mental health services (*May Subd Geog*)

--Migrations

♦--Miscellanea

--Missions (*May Subd Geog*)

--Money (*May Subd Geog*)

--Monuments (*May Subd Geog*)

--Mortality

--Museums (*May Subd Geog*)

♦--Music

♦--Music--Bibliography

♦--Music--Discography

--Music--History and criticism

--Name

♦--Newspapers

--Nutrition

♦--Obituaries

--Origin

♦--Outlines, syllabi, etc.

--Pastoral counseling of (*May Subd Geog*)

--Pensions (*May Subd Geog*)

--Physiology

♦--Pictorial works

♦--Poetry

--Politics and government

--Politics and government--16th century

--Politics and government--17th century

--Politics and government--18th century

--Politics and government--19th century

--Politics and government--20th century

--Population

◆--Portraits

◆--Posters

◆--Prayer-books and devotions

--Promotions (*May Subd Geog*)

--Prophecies

--Psychological testing (*May Subd Geog*)

--Psychology

--Public opinion

--Public welfare (*May Subd Geog*)

--Queens

◆--Quotations

--Race identity

--Recreation (*May Subd Geog*)

◆--Registers

--Rehabilitation (*May Subd Geog*)

--Religion

--Relocation (*May Subd Geog*)

--Research (*May Subd Geog*)

--Respite care (*May Subd Geog*)

--Retirement

--Rites and ceremonies

--Scholarships, fellowships, etc. (*May Subd Geog*)

--Services for (*May Subd Geog*)

--Sexual behavior

--Social conditions

--Social conditions--16th century

--Social conditions--17th century

--Social conditions--18th century

--Social conditions--19th century

--Social conditions--20th century

--Social life and customs

--Social life and customs--16th century

--Social life and customs--17th century

--Social life and customs--18th century

--Social life and customs--19th century

--Social life and customs--20th century

--Social networks (*May Subd Geog*)

--Socialization

--Societies, etc.

♦--Songs and music

--Sports

--Statistical services

♦--Statistics

♦--Statistics, Vital

--Study and teaching (*May Subd Geog*)

--Substance use (*May Subd Geog*)

--Suffrage (*May Subd Geog*)

--Suicidal behavior (*May Subd Geog*)

--Supplementary employment (*May Subd Geog*)

--Surgery (*May Subd Geog*)

--Taxation (*May Subd Geog*)

♦ --Telephone directories

--Time management (*May Subd Geog*)

--Tobacco use (*May Subd Geog*)

--Transportation (*May Subd Geog*)

--Trapping (*May Subd Geog*)

--Travel (*May Subd Geog*)

--Warfare (*May Subd Geog*)

--Wars (*May Subd Geog*)

--Wounds and injuries (*May Subd Geog*)

附錄七：職業類別之下的複分
(Free-floating subdivisions under classes of persons)

　　--Abstracting and indexing (*May Subd Geog*)

◆--Abstracts

　　--Abuse of (*May Subd Geog*)

　　--Alcohol use (*May Subd Geog*)

◆--Anecdotes

◆--Anecdotes

　　--Anniversaries, etc.

　　--Anthropometry (*May Subd Geog*)

◆--Archives

　　--Assaults against (*May Subd Geog*)

　　--Attitudes

◆--Autographs

◆--Bibliography

◆--Biography--Pictorial works

　　--Bonding (*May Subd Geog*)

◆--Book reviews

◆--Books and reading

　　--Care (*May Subd Geog*)

◆--Caricatures and cartoons

◆--Case studies

　　--Certification (*May Subd Geog*)

--Charitable contributions (*May Subd Geog*)

--Civil rights (*May Subd Geog*)

◆--Classification

--Collectibles (*May Subd Geog*)

--Colonization (*May Subd Geog*)

◆--Comic books, strips, etc.

--Conduct of life

◆--Correspondence

--Costume (*May Subd Geog*)

--Counseling of (*May Subd Geog*)

--Crimes against (*May Subd Geog*)

--Death

--Deinstitutionalization (*May Subd Geog*)

--Dental care (*May Subd Geog*)

◆--Diaries

◆--Directories

--Discipline

◆--Discography

--Diseases (*May Subd Geog*)

--Dismissal of (*May Subd Geog*)

◆--Drama

--Drug testing (*May Subd Geog*)

--Drug use (*May Subd Geog*)

--Dwellings (*May Subd Geog*)

◆--Early works to 1800

--Economic conditions

--Economic conditions--16th century

--Economic conditions--17th century

--Economic conditions--18th century

--Economic conditions--19th century

--Economic conditions--20th century

--Education (*May Subd Geog*)

--Education (Continuing education) (*May Subd Geog*)

--Education (Early childhood) (*May Subd Geog*)

--Education (Elementary) (*May Subd Geog*)

--Education (Graduate) (*May Subd Geog*)

--Education (Higher) (*May Subd Geog*)

--Education (Middle school) (*May Subd Geog*)

--Education (Preschool) (*May Subd Geog*)

--Education (Primary) (*May Subd Geog*)

--Education (Secondary) (*May Subd Geog*)

--Effect of automations on (*May Subd Geog*)

--Effect of technological innovations on (*May Subd Geog*)

--Employment (*May Subd Geog*)

--Employment--Foreign countries

--Examinations

♦--Examinations, questions, etc.

♦--Exhibitions

--Family relationships

--Fees

♦--Fiction

--Finance, Personal

♦--Folklore

♦--Genealogy

--Government policy (*May Subd Geog*)

♦--Handbooks, manuals, etc.

--Health and hygiene (*May Subd Geog*)

--Health risk assessment (*May Subd Geog*)

--Historiography

--History

--History--16th century

--History--17th century

--History--18th century

--History--19th century

--History--20th century

♦--History--Sources

--Home care (*May Subd Geog*)

--Homes and haunts (*May Subd Geog*)

--Hospice care (*May Subd Geog*)

--Hospital care (*May Subd Geog*)

--Hospitals (*May Subd Geog*)

--Housing (*May Subd Geog*)

♦--Humor

--Identification

--In-service training (*May Subd Geog*)

♦--Indexes

--Information services

--Institutional care (*May Subd Geog*)

--Insurance requirements (*May Subd Geog*)

--Intellectual life

--Intellectual life--16th century

　　--Intellectual life--17th century

　　--Intellectual life--18th century

　　--Intellectual life--19th century

　　--Intellectual life--20th century

　　--Intelligence levels (*May Subd Geog*)

　　--Intelligence testing (*May Subd Geog*)

◆--Interviews

◆--Job descriptions (*May Subd Geog*)

　　--Job satisfaction (*May Subd Geog*)

　　--Job stress (*May Subd Geog*)

◆--Juvenile drama

◆--Juvenile fiction

◆--Juvenile humor

◆--Juvenile poetry

　　--Language

　　--Legal status, laws, etc. (*May Subd Geog*)

　　--Library resources

　　--Licenses (*May Subd Geog*)

◆--Life skills guides

◆--Literary collections

　　--Long-term care (*May Subd Geog*)

◆--Longitudinal studies

　　--Manuscripts

　　--Medals (*May Subd Geog*)

　　--Medical care (*May Subd Geog*)

　　--Medical examinations (*May Subd Geog*)

　　--Mental health (*May Subd Geog*)

--Mental health services (*May Subd Geog*)

♦--Miscellanea

--Monuments (*May Subd Geog*)

--Mortality

--Museums (*May Subd Geog*)

--Nursing home care (*May Subd Geog*)

--Nutrition

♦--Obituaries

♦--Outlines, syllabi, etc.

--Pastoral counseling of (*May Subd Geog*)

--Pensions (*May Subd Geog*)

--Pensions--Cost-of-living adjustments (*May Subd Geog*)

--Pensions--Effect of inflation on (*May Subd Geog*)

--Pensions--Unclaimed benefits

--Physiology

♦--Pictorial works

♦--Poetry

--Political activity

♦--Portraits

♦--Posters

♦--Prayer-books and devotions

--Professional ethics (*May Subd Geog*)

--Promotions (*May Subd Geog*)

--Prophecies

--Protection (*May Subd Geog*)

--Psychological testing (*May Subd Geog*)

--Psychology

--Public opinion

♦ --Quotations

--Rating of (*May Subd Geog*)

--Recreation (*May Subd Geog*)

--Recruiting (*May Subd Geog*)

♦ --Registers

--Rehabilitation (*May Subd Geog*)

--Reinstatement (*May Subd Geog*)

--Religious life (*May Subd Geog*)

--Relocation (*May Subd Geog*)

--Reporting to (*May Subd Geog*)

--Research (*May Subd Geog*)

--Residence requirements (*May Subd Geog*)

--Resignation (*May Subd Geog*)

--Respite care (*May Subd Geog*)

--Retirement

--Salaries, etc. (*May Subd Geog*)

--Salaries, etc.--Cost-of-living adjustments (*May Subd Geog*)

--Scholarships, fellowships, etc. (*May Subd Geog*)

--Selection and appointment (*May Subd Geog*)

--Services for (*May Subd Geog*)

--Sexual behavior

--Social conditions

--Social conditions--16th century

--Social conditions--17th century

--Social conditions--18th century

--Social conditions--19th century

--Social conditions--20th century

--Social life and customs

--Social life and customs--16th century

--Social life and customs--17th century

--Social life and customs--18th century

--Social life and customs--19th century

--Social life and customs--20th century

--Social networks (*May Subd Geog*)

--Societies, etc.

--Societies and clubs

◆--Songs and music

--Statistical services

◆--Statistics

--Study and teaching (*May Subd Geog*)

--Substance use (*May Subd Geog*)

--Suffrage (*May Subd Geog*)

--Suicidal behavior (*May Subd Geog*)

--Supplementary employment (*May Subd Geog*)

--Supply and demand (*May Subd Geog*)

--Surgery (*May Subd Geog*)

--Surgery--Complications (*May Subd Geog*)

--Surgery--Risk factors (*May Subd Geog*)

--Suspension (*May Subd Geog*)

--Taxation (*May Subd Geog*)

◆--Telephone directories

◆--Terminology

--Time management (*May Subd Geog*)

--Titles

--Tobacco use (*May Subd Geog*)

--Tombs

--Training of (*May Subd Geog*)

--Transfer

--Transportation (*May Subd Geog*)

--Travel (*May Subd Geog*)

--Uniforms

--Vocational guidance (*May Subd Geog*)

--Workload (*May Subd Geog*)

--Wounds and injuries (*May Subd Geog*)

附錄八：一般通用的形式及內容複分

◆--Abbreviations

◆--Abbreviations of titles

--Ability testing (*May Subd Geog*)

--Abstracting and indexing (*May Subd Geog*)

◆--Abstract

--Access control (*May Subd Geog*)

--Accidents (*May Subd Geog*)

--Accidents--Investigation (*May Subd Geog*)

--Accounting

--Accreditation

◆--Acronyms

--Accreditation (*May Subd Geog*)

--Administration

◆--Aerial photographs

--Air conditioning (*May Subd Geog*)

--Air conditioning--Control (*May Subd Geog*)

◆--Amateurs' manuals

--Analysis

◆--Anecdotes

--Anniversaries, etc.

--Archival resources

◆--Archives

♦--Art

♦--Atlases

--Audio-visual aids

♦--Audio-visual aids--Catalogs

♦--Audiotape catalogs

--Auditing

--Authorship

--Automatic control

--Automation

--Autonomous communities

--Awards (***May Subd Geog***)

--Biblical teaching

♦--Bibliography

♦--Bibliography--Catalogs

♦--Bibliography--Early

♦--Bibliography--Exhibitions

--Bibliography--Methodology

♦--Bibliography--Microform catalogs

♦--Bibliography--Union lists

♦--Bibliography of bibliographies

♦--Bio-bibliography

♦--Biography

♦--Biography--Dictionaries

--Biography--History and criticism

♦--Book reviews

--Buildings

♦--By-laws

--By-products

♦--Calendars

--Calibration (*May Subd Geog*)

--Cantons

♦--Caricatures and cartoons

♦--Case studies

♦--Catalogs

♦--Catalogs and collections (*May Subd Geog*)

♦--CD-ROM catalogs

--Censorship (*May Subd Geog*)

--Centennial celebrations, etc.

--Certification (*May Subd Geog*)

--Charitable contributions (*May Subd Geog*)

♦--Charts, diagrams, etc.

♦--Chronology

--Citizen participation

♦--Classification

--Cleaning

♦--Code numbers

♦--Code words

--Cold weather conditions

--Collectibles (*May Subd Geog*)

--Collection and preservation

--Collectors and collecting (*May Subd Geog*)

--Colonies

♦--Comic books, strips, etc.

--Communication systems

♦ --Compact disc catalogs

　--Comparative method

♦ --Comparative studies

　--Competitions (*May Subd Geog*)

　--Composition

　--Computer-aided design (*May Subd Geog*)

　--Computer-assisted instruction

♦ --Computer games

　--Computer network resources

　--Computer networks (*May Subd Geog*)

　--Computer networks--Security measures (*May Subd Geog*)

　--Computer programs

　--Computer simulation

♦ --Concordances

♦ --Congresses

　--Congresses--Attendance

　--Conservation and restoration (*May Subd Geog*)

　--Control (*May Subd Geog*)

♦ --Controversial literature

　--Cooling (*May Subd Geog*)

　--Corrosion (*May Subd Geog*)

　--Corrupt practices (*May Subd Geog*)

　--Cost control

　--Cost effectiveness

　--Cost of operation

　--Costs

♦ --Cross-cultural studies

--Cult (*May Subd Geog*)

♦--Curricula

--Customer services (*May Subd Geog*)

--Data processing

♦--Data tape catalogs

♦--Databases

--Dating

--Decision making

--Defects (*May Subd Geog*)

--Defects--Reporting (*May Subd Geog*)

--Defense measures (*May Subd Geog*)

--Departments

--Design

--Design and construction

♦--Designs and plans

--Deterioration

♦--Dictionaries

♦--Dictionaries--French, 〔Italian, etc.〕

♦--Dictionaries--Polyglot

♦--Dictionaries,Juvenile

♦--Directories

--Discipline

♦--Discography

--Documentation (*May Subd Geog*)

♦--Drama

♦--Drawings

--Drying (*May Subd Geog*)

--Dust control (*May Subd Geog*)

♦--Early works to 1800

--Econometric models

--Economic aspects (*May Subd Geog*)

--Electromechanical analogies

--Employees

♦--Encyclopedias

♦--Encyclopedias, Juvenile

--Endowments

--Energy conservation (*May Subd Geog*)

--Energy consumption (*May Subd Geog*)

--Environmental aspects (*May Subd Geog*)

--Equipment and supplies

--Estimates (*May Subd Geog*)

--Evaluation

--Examinations

♦--Examinations--Study guides

♦--Examinations, questions, etc.

♦--Exhibitions

--Experiments

♦--Facsimiles

♦--Fiction

--Field work

♦--Film catalogs

--Finance

--Fires and fire prevention (*May Subd Geog*)

♦--Folklore

−−Food service (*May Subd Geog*)

−−Forecasting

−−Foreign countries

−−Foreign influences

−−Forgeries (*May Subd Geog*)

◆−−Forms

−−Fume control (*May Subd Geog*)

−−Government policy (*May Subd Geog*)

−−Grading (*May Subd Geog*)

−−Graphic methods

◆−−Guidebooks

◆−−Handbooks, manuals, etc.

−−Health aspects (*May Subd Geog*)

−−Heating and ventilation (*May Subd Geog*)

−−Heating and ventilation−−Control (*May Subd Geog*)

−−Heraldry

−−Historiography

−−History

−−History−−To 1500

−−History−−16th century

−−History−−17th century

−−History−−18th century

−−History−−19th century

−−History−−20th century

◆−−History−−Chronology

−−History−−Philosophy

◆−−History−−Sources

　　--History and criticism

　　--History of doctrines

　　--History of doctrines--Early church, ca. 30-600

　　--History of doctrines--Middle Ages, 600-1500

　　--History of doctrines--16th century

　　--History of doctrines--17th century

　　--History of doctrines--18th century

　　--History of doctrines--19th century

　　--History of doctrines--20th century

　　--Hot weather conditions (*May Subd Geog*)

♦--Humor

　　--Identification

♦--Illustrations

　　--In art

♦--Indexes

　　--Industrial applications (*May Subd Geog*)

　　--Influence

　　--Information resources

　　--Information services

　　--Insignia

　　--Inspection (*May Subd Geog*)

　　--Instruments

♦--Interactive multimedia

　　--International cooperation

　　--Interpretation

♦--Inventories

♦--Job descriptions (*May Subd Geog*)

◆－－Juvenile drama

◆－－Juvenile fiction

◆－－Juvenile films

◆－－Juvenile humor

◆－－Juvenile literature

◆－－Juvenile poetry

◆－－Juvenile software

◆－－Juvenile sound recordings

－－Labeling (*May Subd Geog*)

－－Labor productivity (*May Subd Geog*)

◆－－Laboratory manuals

－－Language

◆－－Legends

－－Library resources

－－Licenses (*May Subd Geog*)

－－Licenses－－Fees (*May Subd Geog*)

－－Lighting (*May Subd Geog*)

－－Linear programming

◆－－Literary collections

－－Location (*May Subd Geog*)

◆－－Longitudinal studies

－－Maintenance and repair

－－Management

－－Manuscripts

◆－－Manuscripts－－Catalogs

◆－－Manuscripts－－Facsimiles

◆－－Manuscripts－－Indexes

♦ −−Manuscripts−−Microform catalogs

♦ −−Maps

♦ −−Maps−−Bibliography

♦ −−Maps−−Early works to 1800

♦ −−Maps−−Facsimiles

　−−Maps−−Symbols

♦ −−Maps, Comparative

♦ −−Maps, Manuscript

♦ −−Maps, Mental

♦ −−Maps, Outline and base

♦ −−Maps, Physical

♦ −−Maps, Pictorial

♦ −−Maps, Toppgraphic

♦ −−Maps, Tourist

♦ −−Maps for children

♦ −−Maps for the blind

♦ −−Maps for the visually handicapped

　−−Marketing

　−−Materials

　−−Mathematical models

　−−Mathematics

　−−Measurement

　−−Medals (*May Subd Geog*)

　−−Medical examinations (*May Subd Geog*)

♦ −−Meditations

　−−Membership

　−−Methodology

♦--Microform catalogs

♦--Miscellanea

--Models (*May Subd Geog*)

--Moisture (*May Subd Geog*)

--Moral and ethical aspects (*May Subd Geog*)

--Museums (*May Subd Geog*)

--Name

--Names

♦--Newspapers

--Noise

♦--Nomenclature

♦--Nomograms

♦--Notation

♦--Observations

♦--Observers' manuals

--Officials and employees

--On postage stamps

♦--Outlines, syllabi, etc.

--Packaging

--Packing (*May Subd Geog*)

♦--Papal documents

♦--Parodies, imitations, etc.

♦--Patents

♦--Periodicals

♦--Periodicals--Abbreviations of titles

♦--Periodicals--Bibliography

♦--Periodicals--Bibliography--Catalogs

◆ーーPeriodicals—Bibliography—Union lists

◆ーーPeriodicals—Indexes

◆ーーPersonal narratives

　ーーPersonnel management

　ーーPhilosophy

◆ーーPhotographs

◆ーーPhotographs from space

　ーーPhysiological aspects

　ーーPhysiological effect

◆ーーPictorial works

　ーーPlanning

◆ーーPoetry

　ーーPolitical activity

　ーーPolitical aspects (*May Subd Geog*)

◆ーーPopular works

◆ーーPosters

　ーーPower supply (*May Subd Geog*)

　ーーPractice (*May Subd Geog*)

◆ーーPrayer-books and devotions

　ーーPrayer-books and devotions—History and criticism

　ーーPreservation (*May Subd Geog*)

　ーーPress coverage (*May Subd Geog*)

　ーーPrevention

　ーーPrices (*May Subd Geog*)

　ーーPrices—Government policy (*May Subd Geog*)

　ーーPrivate collections (*May Subd Geog*)

　ーーPrivileges and immunities

♦ --Problems, exercises, etc.

--Production control (*May Subd Geog*)

--Production standards (*May Subd Geog*)

♦ --Programmed instruction

--Programming

--Prophecies

--Protection (*May Subd Geog*)

--Provinces

--Psychological aspects

--Psychology

--Public opinion

--Publishing (*May Subd Geog*)

--Purchasing (*May Subd Geog*)

--Quality control

♦ --Quotations, maxims, etc.

--Rates (*May Subd Geog*)

♦ --Records and correspondence

--Recreational use

--Regions

♦ --Registers

--Reliability

--Religion

--Remodeling

--Remote sensing

♦ --Remote-sensing maps

--Repairing (*May Subd Geog*)

--Republics

--Research (*May Subd Geog*)

--Research grants (*May Subd Geog*)

◆--Reviews

◆--Romances

◆--Rules

◆--Rules and practice

--Safety appliances (*May Subd Geog*)

--Safety measures

◆--Safety regulations (*May Subd Geog*)

--Sanitation (*May Subd Geog*)

--Scholarships, fellowships, etc. (*May Subd Geog*)

--Scientific applications (*May Subd Geog*)

--Security measures (*May Subd Geog*)

◆--Sermons

--Sex differences

--Simulation methods

--Slang

◆--Slides

--Social aspects (*May Subd Geog*)

--Societies, etc.

--Sociological aspects

◆--Software

◆--Songs and music

◆--Sources

◆--Specifications (*May Subd Geog*)

◆--Specimens

--Spectra

◆ ――Speeches in Congress

――Stability

――Standards (*May Subd Geog*)

――State supervision

――States

――Statistical methods

――Statistical services

◆ ――Statistics

――Storage (*May Subd Geog*)

――Study and teaching (*May Subd Geog*)

――Study and teaching――Activity programs (*May Subd Geog*)

――Study and teaching――Audio-visual aids

――Study and teaching――Simulation methods

――Study and teaching――Supervision (*May Subd Geog*)

――Study and teaching (Continuing education) (*May Subd Geog*)

――Study and teaching (Continuing education)――Audio-visual aids

――Study and teaching (Early childhood) (*May Subd Geog*)

――Study and teaching (Early childhood)――Activity programs (*May Subd Geog*)

――Study and teaching (Early childhood)――Audio-visual aids

――Study and teaching (Elementary) (*May Subd Geog*)

――Study and teaching (Elementary)――Activity programs (*May Subd Geog*)

――Study and teaching (Elementary)――Audio-visual aids

――Study and teaching (Elementary)――Simulation methods

――Study and teaching (Graduate) (*May Subd Geog*)

――Study and teaching (Higher) (*May Subd Geog*)

――Study and teaching (Higher)――Activity programs (*May Subd Geog*)

――Study and teaching (Higher)――Audio-visual aids

--Study and teaching (Higher)--Simulation methods

--Study and teaching (Internship) (*May Subd Geog*)

--Study and teaching (Middle school) (*May Subd Geog*)

--Study and teaching (Middle school)--Audio-visual aids

--Study and teaching (Preschool) (*May Subd Geog*)

--Study and teaching (Preschool)--Activity programs (*May Subd Geog*)

--Study and teaching (Preschool)--Audio-visual aids

--Study and teaching (Primary) (*May Subd Geog*)

--Study and teaching (Primary)--Activity programs (*May Subd Geog*)

--Study and teaching (Primary)--Audio-visual aids

--Study and teaching (Residency) (*May Subd Geog*)

--Study and teaching (Secondary) (*May Subd Geog*)

--Study and teaching (Secondary)--Activity programs (*May Subd Geog*)

--Study and teaching (Secondary)--Audio-visual aids

--Study and teaching (Secondary)--Simulation methods

♦--Study guides

♦--Tables

--Taxation (*May Subd Geog*)

--Technique

--Technological innovations (*May Subd Geog*)

♦--Telephone directories

♦--Terminology

--Terminology--Pronunciation

--Territories and possessions

--Testing

--Textbooks

♦--Texts

--Themes, motives

--Therapeutic use (*May Subd Geog*)

◆--Tombs

--Toxicology (*May Subd Geog*)

◆--Trademarks

--Translating

◆--Translations

◆--Translations into 〔name of language〕

◆--Translations into 〔name of language〕 --Bibliography

--Transportation (*May Subd Geog*)

--Tropical conditions

◆--Union lists

--Union territories

--Validity

--Valuation (*May Subd Geog*)

--Vibration (*May Subd Geog*)

◆--Video catalogs

--Vocational guidance (*May Subd Geog*)

--Waste disposal (*May Subd Geog*)

--Waste minimization (*May Subd Geog*)

--Water-supply

--Weight

--Weights and measures

附錄九：《主題編目手冊：主題標目》大綱

VOLUME ONE

H1185	Religions
	Religious Bodies
H1186	Religious and Monastic Orders
H1187	Christian Denominations
H1188	Sacred Works
	Vehicles
H1195	Land Vehicles
H1200	Wars

VOLUME THREE

Special Topics, Materials, Subdivisions, Etc.

H1205	Abstracts
H1206.5	Acronyms
H1210	Addresses, Essays, Lectures
H1210.5	Aerial and Space Photography
H1211	Airports
H1223	Arabs
H1225	Archaeological Works
H1230	Archives and Archival Resources
H1250	Art and Fine Art
H1255	Artistic Photography
H1265	Awards
H1285	Battles
H1295	Bible: Special Topics
H1300	Bible: Versions
H1322	Bibliographies about Individual Persons

H1325	Bibliography of Bibliographies
H1328	Bio-bibliography
H1330	Biography
H1332	Biological Names
H1333	Books and Reading
H1333.5	Boundaries
H1334	Buildings and Other Structures
H1334.5	Buildings and Structures in Cities: Assignment of Headings
H1350	Case Studies and Cases
H1360	Catalogs
H1361	Catalogs of Library Materials
H1365	Cemeteries
H1366	Census
H1367	Chronology
H1370	Civilization
H1412	Classical and Ancient Works
H1425	Collected Works and Collections
H1427	Collections of Objects
H1430	Comics and Comic Characters
H1435	Commentaries on Individual Works
H1438	Composers and Works about Music of Individual Composers
H1460	Congresses
H1465	Constitutions
H1468	Contracts
H1472	Controversial Literature
H1475	Cooking and Cookbooks
H1480	Correspondence of Individual Persons

H1510	Cross-Cultural Studies
H1520	Databases
H1530	Description and Travel
H1532	Design and Construction
H1538	Diaries
H1540	Dictionaries
H1550	Digests
H1558	Directories
H1560	Disasters, Riots, Demonstrations, Etc.
H1564	Discovery and Exploration
H1570	Dissertations and Theses
H1574	Dynasties, Royal Houses, Etc.
H1576	Early Works
H1578	Economic Conditions
H1579	Education
H1580	Effect of One Topic on Another
H1580.5	Electronic Serials
H1581	Emigration and Immigration
H1591	Evaluation
H1592	Events
H1593	Exhibitions
H1595	Facsimiles
H1600	Festschriften
H1610	Fictitious Characters
H1624	Finance
H1627	Folklore
H1628	Forecasting

H1629	Foreign Relations
H1630	Gazetteers
H1631	Genealogy
H1636	Gods of Greek and Roman Mythology
H1642	Government Policy
H1643	Government Publications
H1645	Guidebooks
H1646	Handbooks, Manuals, Etc.
H1647	History
H1659	Illustrations
H1660	Imprints
H1670	Indexes
H1673	Industries Based on Products
H1675	Influence of One Topic on Another
H1675.5	Information Services
H1676	Inquisition
H1676.5	Inspection
H1678	Interviews
H1680	Islam
H1690	Juvenile Materials
H1705	Legal Materials: Law and Legislation and Other Subdivisions
H1710	Legal Materials: Legal Research
H1715	Legal Materials: Legislation
H1720	Legends and Stories about Animals
H1775	Literature: General
H1780	Literature: Drama
H1790	Literature: Fiction

H1795	Literature: Legends and Romances
H1800	Literature: Poetry
H1828	Literature from One Place in Multiple Languages
H1845	Local History and Genealogical Source Materials
H1848	Longitudinal Studies
H1855	Manuscripts
H1865	Maps and Atlases
H1870	Marketing
H1890	Mental Health and Mental Health Services
H1893	Microforms
H1895	Miniature Books

VOLUME FOUR

Special Topics, Materials, Subdivisions, Etc.

H1910	Miscellanea
H1916	Museums
H1916.3	Music: General
H1916.5	Music: Jazz and Popular Music
H1917	Music of Ethnic, National, and Religious Groups
H1917.5	Music Form/Genre Headings: Medium of Performance
H1919	Name and Names
H1919.5	Nationalities
H1920	Newspapers on Special Topics and Ethnic Newspapers
H1925	Parks, Reserves, National Monuments, Etc.
H1927	Periodicals
H1928	Personal Narratives

H1929	Philosophy
H1935	Pictorial Works
H1942	Politics and Government
H1943.5	Popular Works
H1945	Postage Stamps on Specific Topics
H1945.5	Posters
H1949	Professional Ethics
H1955	Public Opinion
H1965	Publishers' Catalogs
H1969	Quotations and Maxims
H1970	Railroads
H1975	Readers
H1980	Referencc Books
H1995	Regimental Histories
H1996	Relations and Military Relations
H1997	Religion
H1998	Religious Aspects of Topics
H2015	Religious Denominations or Religions as Subdivisions
H2015.5	Religious Life
H2016	Religious Life and Customs
H2020	Research
H2021	Reviews
H2032	Sermons
H2040	Simulation Methods in Special Fields
H2055	Social Conditions
H2057	Social Life and Customs
H2060	Societies

H2070	Software and Works about Software
H2075	Songs and Music
H2080	Sources
H2083	Specifications
H2095	Statistics
H2098	Streets and Roads
H2100	Strikes and Lockouts
H2110	Study and Teaching
H2145	Supplementary Works
H2149	Surveys
H2160	Tables
H2184	Terms and Phrases
H2185	Territories and Possessions
H2186	Testing
H2187	Textbooks
H2190	Texts
H2217	Training
H2219	Translating
H2220	Translations
H2225	Transportation
H2227	Treaties
H2228	Trials
H2230	Visual Materials and Non-Music Sound Recordings
H2232	Vocational Guidance
H2400	Yearbooks

英漢詞語對照索引表

A

G

H

I

J

K

L

M

S

漢英詞語對照索引表

一畫

二畫

四畫

五畫

六畫

七畫

八畫

九畫

十二畫

十三畫

十四畫

十五畫

十六畫

十七畫

十八畫

十九畫

二十三畫

大雅叢刊書目

法學叢書書目

生活法律漫談

輕鬆學習美國法律	鄧 穎 懋	著
老師的法律責任	沈 銀 和	著
主任與職員的法律責任	沈 銀 和	著

圖書資訊學叢書書目

美國國會圖書館主題編目（增訂版）	陳 麥 麟 屏 林 國 強	著	排版中
圖書資訊組織原理	何 光 國	著	
圖書資訊學導論	周 寧 森	著	
文獻計量學導論	何 光 國	著	
現代化圖書館管理	李 華 偉 景 懿 頻	著	
圖書館與當代資訊科技	楊 宗 英 李 燦 傳	著	
圖書館學理論基礎	何 光 國	著	排版中

教育叢書書目

西洋教育思想史	林玉体	臺灣師大	已出版
西洋教育史	林玉体	臺灣師大	撰稿中
教育社會學	宋明順	臺灣師大	撰稿中
課程發展	梁恒正	臺灣師大	撰稿中
教育哲學	楊深坑	臺灣師大	撰稿中
電腦補助教學	邱貴發	臺灣師大	撰稿中
教材教法	張新仁	高雄師大	撰稿中
教育評鑑	秦夢群	政治大學	撰稿中
高等教育	陳舜芬	臺灣大學	撰稿中

中國現代史叢書書目 （張玉法主編）

中國托派史	唐寶林	著	中國社科院
學潮與戰後中國政治(1945~1949)	廖風德	著	政治大學
商會與中國早期現代化	虞和平	著	中國社科院
歷史地理學與現代中國史學	彭明輝	著	政治大學
西安事變新探 ——張學良與中共關係之研究	楊奎松	著	中國社科院
抗戰史論	蔣永敬	著	政治大學
漢語與中國新文化啟蒙	周光慶 劉　瑋	著	華中師大
美國與中國政治(1917~1928) ——以南北分裂政局為中心的探討	吳翎君	著	中央研究院
抗戰初期的遠東國際關係	王建朗	著	中國社科院
從接收到淪陷 ——戰後平津地區接收工作之檢討	林桶法	著	輔仁大學
中共與莫斯科的關係(1920~1960)	楊奎松	著	中國社科院
近代中國銀行與企業的關係 (1897~1945)	李一翔	著	上海社科院
蔣介石與希特勒 ——民國時期的中德關係	馬振犢 戚如高	著	中國第二歷 史檔案館
北京政府與國際聯盟 (1919~1928)	唐啟華	著	中興大學
近代中國民主政治發展史	張玉法	著	中央研究院

三民大專用書書目——教育